Collected Poems
1955-2015

JOHN WOOLLEY

Collected
Poems

1955-2015

WITH A PREFACE
BY PETER SCUPHAM

STONE TROUGH
BOOKS

Books by the same author:

Deliver me from Safety (1994)

Cars Looked Peculiar (2010)

(Edits) *As it was in the Beginning* (2011)

Walking to Hagetmau (2014)

ISBN 978-0-9929497-3-0

Published by Stone Trough Books
The Old Rectory
Settrington, York
YO17 8NP

Printed by Jetprint, Whitby

For Sylvie

Preface

JOHN WOOLLEY's poems have been caviar to the general, simply because he has never cared to hustle and jostle his poems into the market-place. They have been produced in small editions *pro amicis suis*, which is delightful, but unfortunate, because these are poems of great distinction which deserve a much wider audience. If they had come Mandeville's way when John Mole and I were publishing contemporary poets, we would have leaped at the chance to have them propped up over our type-cabinet while we set them letterpress! Here are some reasons why they would have so excited us.

Auden, one of John Woolley's masters, and a Yorkshireman, though not as complete a Yorkshireman (and certainly not such a loving Francophile), asks of a poem what kind of contraption it is, and what kind of guy inhabits the contraption. John's poems are formal structures—he is perfectly adept at all the tricks of the trade, sestinas, villanelles, what have you—and his longer poems have a certainty of structure, an architecture which compels confidence. And whatever the present currency of the word, they are, as Auden's poems are, civilized, being humane, rooted in a deep understanding of the history and culture of the two nations he loves—his wife is French—and deeply bedded into the contrasting landscapes of Southern France and the North Yorkshire moorland around Whitby, the town where John lives, and where he was born in 1936. This cultural background is deepened by a strong sense of the bones and formation of landscape, and a delighted knowledge, laid down early in life, of the creatures—particularly the birds—which bring landscape into life and song.

John's own personality is always present—the observant, loving, amused watcher—but it never calls attention to itself. The poems are firmly rooted in the other, that transient, wonderful pageant which lights up these poems without overburdening them.

Perhaps it is possible, without being much of a subscriber to practical criticism, to give a few examples of the kind of writing which should compel admiration, even in so louche and self-referential an age as ours. John has written several poems centred loosely on the works of Jean Giono, the French novelist from Haute-Provence, best known in England for his novella *The Man Who Planted Trees* but widely regarded in France as the greatest French novelist of the second half of the Twentieth Century. These lines are from the third and seventh stanzas of the Giono sequence 'Spring':

> Thin streaks of rain hung on the gale in shawls.
> Like hair from a goat's belly. Overnight
> The wind sang in the woods, and went out like a light.

Then creaturely life gathers its own momentum with the warming season, and

>   ... the blood
> Began its questioning, its pursuing,
> Through golden lattices and gilded floods
> Of twilight, the schmaltzy paths of feeling:
> Lovecalls beside the swollen river's thundering

It is no easy thing to write with such forceful, assured and controlled energy. But though this is a poetry rich in suggestion, delighting in the wayward and surprising effects of language, there are poems whose lucid celebration of simply what *is* are a reminder that poetry, as the observant Geoffrey Grigson knew, can celebrate the transient, subduing metaphor to the actual, as in these lines from *Venelles*:

> I wanted to catch the purple of hills,
> The soft shrill of crickets reproaching night,
> Snowclusters of snails on waving sedges,
> And the chuckle of sheepbells faraway.

Sensation, though, in John's poems rides tandem with the intelligence, the alert, considering, mind, which is where, perhaps, in poems like 'Courances,' where the water-gardens of the Château become the subject of an easy button-holing conversation, the reader is invited to consider, among other things, cleanliness, the narcissism of reflection, the fountains of Persepolis and Xanadu, an amused correspondence between Boileau and Le Nôtre, critic and garden designer, an aqueduct driven through Samos—and yet, as in Auden's landscape poems, there is no strain, simply a civilized voice exploring and clarifying the restful geometries of water:

> You can be here alone
> Or surrounded by people but still you must marvel
>
> How everything seamlessly wanders from vista
> To vista and always with water behind. Le Nôtre
> Might not have read Heraclitus but somebody must.

All our landscapes are landscapes of the mind, and it is not always possible to go to Courances or Ronas Voe, the sea-inlet on Shetland which John celebrates in a stunning series of sonnets to his wife, Sylvie. Leonardo da Vinci could bring complex, inhabited landscapes to life from the stains and cracks on a peeling wall, and I once asked my bed-bound father in illness how he spent the time. 'Oh, just go for walks,' came the reply. So John Woolley, who has become very familiar with the odd time-continuum of hospital life, has a delightful poem on the ward curtains whose colours and streaks resolve themselves into John's known and loved Yorkshire landscapes; a time when the nights are for listening to Bach cantatas, a music 'dropped straight from Elysia' and fitful sleep produces a wonderful quartet of dream poems where he finds himself hovering between France and an English hospital, 'writing strange music for hammerless/Harpsichords' among artistic friends in a spin of bizarre creativity, pondering a mysterious white grime encasing books in 'Daleside Castle Library', or finding himself and his family caught up in a Paris coup under Louis-Phillipe. As is customary with John, we are given an enticing combination of knowledge, half-amused imaginative distancing, and a generous understanding of his fellow-patients, the hospital staff, the affection his visitors bring. There have been some fine sequences about the alternative world sickness opens doors into, by Clive James, Hugo Williams and John Mole. These poems, entirely devoid of self-pity, make a notable addition to that canon.

Always so much more to say about poems which distil a lifetime's experiences, and so readers must discover for themselves the affectionate tributes to friends and relations, the vivid childhood memories, the humoresques and pieces of diablerie which enliven the collection. Enough to say that I have rarely enjoyed making the acquaintance of a contemporary poet more than when I was given the chance to read and re-read these individual, handsome and necessary poems.

PETER SCUPHAM

Contents

Recollection
(2008)

Sandsend 1945

That day, which I am not good at remembering,
Being in August, must have been holiday,
And my family, though in mourning
For Grampa, might have mentioned Enola Gay,

But I do not remember. Games on the sands
With a bucket and spade, perhaps, but no capers
Like we had had for Germany. And
Only one picture on all the papers.

They piece and ravel and argue now the saga
And I read it, and wonder what I was told –
That day they went to Hiroshima
        I was nine years old
                But I do not remember.

Civil Defence, Stroud 1956

'There will be many deaths, like at
'Iroshima: don't save the dead!'
(Save the quick?) 'A body squashed flat
Is presumably dead,' they said,
'Well, leave it; get used to the smell
Of death and gas. Do not forget
There 'as been an explosion: well
People will suffer from shock. Get
What the eye doesn't see, below
Shattered débris, alive, not dead.
This sort of problem most of you
Are likely to be confronted
With. Remember that the technique
Of rescue comes in five main 'Ifs'
And do not waste bandage.' (Or seek
For the living among the stiffs?)
'Save time and save life, this is advice
Which must be emphasized.' (It sticks:
What's worth saying, they don't say twice
But, like Chaucer, at least times six.)

American Cemetery, Madingley

The dead lie under the long sod's rule
In perfect formation, dressed by the right.
Tinker by tailor, scholar by fool,
That drowned their books and buried their spite,
Disowned themselves and marched unto the camp.

Will march no longer.

                    But will stamp
Stamp at judgement, though they cannot dance;
Will stamp—one two—bending their knees:
The dead will advance
                 and stand at ease.

Old Man in Savoie

When the snows melted
They washed away half of his house.
Great crooked stones, resting together,
But draughty as hell
Fell with a rumble
Of breaking monuments.

It was the same, he said,
When the soldiers came,
Over the mountains with artillery.

Now he sits in a little wooden hut
By the side of the alpine road
And sells sweet liqueur—hot
With the fragrance of lavender:
'C'est le genépi, M'sieur,
  C'est le genépi'—
Telling you gently, because you are foreign
Like the soldiers.
'Non M'sieur, je n'ai pas d'enfants
Les soldats les ont tués.'

Le Bec-Hellouin

Oh yes the blackbirds sing, even in the city.
At daylight the sun filters warm through my curtains,
But when your letter comes, post-marked from Brionne,
For a moment, I am a thousand years younger.

In a white church, the nuns' high sweet voices
Are filtering into the valley woods
—Blackbirds can only compete while they pray—
But what are they praying for? But to live
Even a moment in this sunhung world…
And then two maidens bring three little girls
To paddle at the water, and they laugh
With high sweet voices; while all surrounding
Trees and rich leaves of lusty Normandy
Bake in the glare, awaiting a moment
When Abelard or Childebert will come
Or Harcourt's master-mason give them shade …

And someone is hammering wood in the garden
And the water is running out of the basin
And someone has found thump-thump on the radio

Thank you for your letter—for a moment anyway.

Illyria

Song

My mouse of virtue slips between
The palings of the wooden laws
And nibbles gently at the green
Of all my lovely metaphors.

She does not stop to choose a path
But plunges through the quavering stalks,
Does not dispute an acted wrath
But leaves the field for me to walk.

The moon is hid, the stars depart,
She kneels upon the lawn and weeps
She curls within my arms, and sleeps,
And nibbles gently at my heart.

Sonet

To know that there are beasts moving quiet-
ly in the night alongside, chewing the
cud and being there endlessly, on sand-
worn stones with a ninety year footstep stuck
in their speechlessness, this is my quiet-
us – our, if you love me, evensong's plinth
for a column of selenite, sea and
sky high and deep, fire and earth clear and muck-
spredden –
       leading us up to the hayloft
where there are ticks and mosquitoes, where, on
the stones, on the beasts' backs, we shall sleep soft-
ly and fearlessly, leaving our reason
float in a column of selenite that
can be exploded but cannot be cut.

The Seacoast of Bohemia

Quid tempestates autumni et sidera dicam ... ? Georgics I
(Why should I speak of the storms and constellations of autumn?)

The life you limit, the saltwind craves
For a brand that kindles the diving tern
As sunshine's good for a sandblown thistle,
The life you limit is starved, and raves,
Till dark on the wastes that the sea uncovered,
Smoothworn driftwood collars the light
And the moon is cold as the sun was brave
And the life you limit is bound in night.

Song

I had a bitter lover
Or that was what he said
I loved him with my body
He loved me with his head

You do not understand me
My clever lover said
Do not confuse Platonic love
With what we do in bed

I do not understand you
My would-be lover cried
It's just co-ordination
                    And
My love as lover died.

Dans le Vaucluse

Mistral roars in the unused terraces
Among the stumps of frozen olive trees
And the débris, husks and carapaces
Of a million dead snails, and the faeces
Of sheep, before coming down on the lee
Of the farm, where brother and sister fold
Their arms in separate tranquillities,
Who lived incestuously but now are old
And piss in the stable where there are no horses.

Mistral roars in the untended grapevine
On higher ground where there is no water
Among rampant hares; and the old dog whines
In his dreams in the kitchen, and whimpers,
But the hunt is over; there is no heir
To the cabbages and glow-worms, the few
Last fields, laid down by a Roman farmer,
Save for a garage mechanic nephew
And the stillborn child she fed one night to the swine.

Mistral roars, in vinestumps black like phantoms,
At dawn, when the old man hawks and labours
Alone, in an air swept clean of problems,
At dusk when toads croak, drinks and remembers
A week he spent in the city—prefers
Money in gold, and the gold is buried,
Untouched, unwanted as olive's silver
And forgotten like that till the will is read
And the nephew will sell and the tractors will come.

Aix-en-Provence

1. Dans la rue du Puits Neuf

I said
I will make a new song this morning
After the deluge in the dark night
There are torrents of sunshine pouring
Over the sheer sides of the roofline.
I walked
Through the steam of the untouched street
Sniffing a mixture of fresh bread
And ground coffee, and putting my feet
In the gaps between babies and turds.
I heard
A classical fanfare, put on by accident,
Hastily cut, to give place to
The coffee cantata. And with this portent
—It is a hymn that I will write—
I said

2. Cours Mirabeau

She sits knitting among excited talk.
Sometimes her eyes flit cautiously to left
Or right, without disturbing her repose,
And the one she considers, the prize bull,
Shifts uneasily in his place, without
Being aware of her regard.

So I have seen the praying mantis
Religiously stalking the long grass
In a devout contemplation of her soul,
Take up her husband in a pure embrace
And bite his head off,
Maintaining a virginal calm.

3. La Boucherie

Here is the cow with the crumpled knees,
Whose brainstruck slumping counteracts on brain,
Cutting the lifeline while the phrases flow.

You cannot call the killer inhumane,
Question the craftsman on the left hindquarter,
Blood-pumping boldly in the unglazed eye;
This is his business and he knows it
And no more asks each death an explanation
Than you ask bakers for a slice of life.

Flesh and fetish fall apart and the knife
Cleaves between clavicle's knuckle, cuts
Away gristle and sinew, gently persuades
Between tissue and tendon and bone,
That in this form gathers
And grows into custom.

       Now hands
Worship the fashion of shaping infallible
Steel actions: loving your victim forms
No part of slaughter, since metal
That's whetted cannot help but cut.

4. Route du Tholonet

Au loin s'étendaient les routes toutes blanches de lune
(Into the distance stretched the road, shining palely in the moonlight)

Zola: La Fortune des Rougon

So cold that one is conscious of each foot
One advances and the stars, if further
Away in this century, tonight are
Near. Tree after tree stands to attention
By the glacial road and the bleached white roots
Distend tortured shadows as headlights roar.
Ice rimes the grass and grips on the handlebars
And the road seems awaiting processions

Of ghosts with a purpose, dancing in time
And out, who are one with the night that throbs
Tiredly and coldly on willow and lime:
Jurors of gypsies, familiars of mobs,
Fantastically present and laughing there:

Which they're not, but the journey seems shorter.

5. Canal Zola
and for Clem Gibson

I know what honeysuckle is
And the taste of honey from lavender,
Mutton fattened on sage and thyme,
 Asparagus and cherries;
  But they're not for ever,
  Or even our lifetime
  Listed as memories;

I know what running water does,
How the dayflow runs cloudily and thick,
Seems to tumble haphazardly
 At nightfall, harmonious
  But not automatic,
  Clearly a melody
  And clearly measureless.

I know how wind-seized olives shake
Dust from blue moths that hover, hover there,
How black fritillaries and bees
 Parading in covies, stake
  Their claim on flowers
  That nod in the same breeze
  Whose pulse we cannot take.

I know how to make reed boats, and
If I show you, this you will remember,
Perhaps as a pointless skill, though
 Evocative. Rivers and
  Rushes grow everywhere,
  But we can never know
  Where our reed boats will land.

6. Venelles
and for Simon

I wanted to catch the purple of hills,
The soft shrill of crickets reproaching night,
Snowclusters of snails on waving sedges,
And the chuckle of sheepbells faraway.
There are five trees on a skyline which fill
My imagination, and a so slight
Flicker of dragonflies' wings on the edge
Of a pond. Enough to be overplayed

And to summon the furies. You, my son,
Who bewail the end of the world, and rage
On the fall of a sparrow, pity one
Moment, me; who have these as heritage,
Which I will squander in too rich splendour
Of a great list, that you may remember.

7. Mont Sainte-Victoire
and for Barney and Edwina

Clear light is starfall but can be achieved
Sudden and sweepingly, broadbanked as grass,
As granite masses sitting in sunshine;
The careless line, the scattering of ink
Is calligraphic, sunfall seems to be weaved
Whatever frolics, motes, thoughts, shortcuts pass
Into action, dark black, rust and carmine
Mean what you imagine and what you think
At that moment, and later, lava, shade,
Autumn and vineyards; neither are these true
Judgements necessities, but a parade
Arrayed, a superfluous retinue.

I will not tell then how that they are gone
Home unto Athens when the play is done.

Pavillon Sévigné

*A bourrée for Marie de Rabutin-Chantal
and Elisabeth François*

Then on our ordered lawn they danced
By moonlight pacing but without the loom
    Of our great chestnut, then, entranced
By when and how precisely their loam feet
    Would carry them over the hills and far,
Far away, to revolve again as meet
    For the Marquise in her sheltered room
And something due to her well-ordered universe.

    Interruption. A countess calls
From Lausanne. Room with bath on the garden
    In June, a front seat in the stalls
For the tinselled repetition. We will hire
    Bourbonnais folkies in the era's
Costume. They will bow and scrape and inspire,
    Perhaps, a jig from our businessmen,
An amusement in the tedium of their cures.

    Enchaînement. Living in comfort,
Even graciously, puts limitations
    On this kind of theme, the thought
Which wanders in a maze of silver trunks
    Incautiously, then something seems to jar
Its progress, which the wild gavotte debunks
    As the ageing Marquise might well have done
When on our ordered lawn they danced their rustic measures.

Inaccessible 1981
and for Alison

Discomfort is taken for granted, rain coming sideways,
Leaking through canvas and wood while we live
On top of each other, sharing the rations.
Noise is continuous. Not just honking of penguin,
Bray of shearwater or banshee wail of as yet
Unidentified fowl but roar, unremitting,
Remorseless of roller, breaker and surf
On a grey-black, shingle-strewn shore which we count
Ourselves lucky to have, like the spring of fresh water.
Behind us, tussock and phylica cling to the face
Of the cliffs but in front there is only the ocean
For anything up to a couple of thousand miles.

The shingle is awkward, pebbles are smooth
But uneven and frequently wet, another good reason
To look where you're putting your feet.
The jetsam is marvellous. What Eliot called
The gear of foreign dead men, mingling
With whale's teeth, sea wrack, unflyblown fishheads
And driftwood of all shapes and sizes can,
Suddenly, metamorphose into penguin, skua
And seal, all alive-o and curious,
Not going anywhere. After all, this is their patch.

You can't see any of this from our single window,
Only the sea and the sky and you'd think
You'd get bored but it's eye-gripping stuff. It's the noise
Which drives one to climb, apart from the pleasure
Of sitting in tree fern and Yorkshire fog,
Surrounded by curious albatrosses,
Looking down on silent ripples of ocean
Moving into a sandless beach. Rarely
We talk to Tristania, which tells us that
England is losing a Test match and Brezhnev
Has died.

      I don't think du Bellay was right
About Ulysses being heureux back in Ithaca;
Happiness lives ahead. What I can see
Now and maybe for ever is two beachcombers,
Linked by a baulk on their shoulders,
Stark on a single line between island and water,
And taking it home because that's where they live.

Otaki

and for Andrew

Just now the puriri's in bloom and the fantails
Flit cheekily, half hidden in foliage, flirt,
Hesitate and disappear. It is hot and one dozes.

To awake, like Banks, to the chimes of the bellbird
Is no longer a real possibility
But Australian magpies do their thing
In the field next door, while chaffinch and thrush
Hog the breadcrumbs on manicured lawn.

Everything grows very fast and the natural flora
When flattened to make room for sheep gives way
To leylandii and gum-trees and gorse
Not to speak of astonishing dry stone walls.

The culture is half-oriental. Castles
And ancient rights of way are alien concepts
Apart from the burial sites of long-gone Maori chiefs,
Who were also at one time intruders.

If one has any regrets, they are only for distant moors
Which re-echo the wind and the peewees crying.

Variations on
Familiar Themes
(2011)

The Marmottan Revisited 2011

I sit wherever there's an empty space
Surrounded by some canvas, framed in wood,
Whose colours, like the viewers, interface,
Shifting and settling in a restless flood.
What would he think, that Irish Maecenas
Who asked for proof that people wanted food
For something more than bellies? Hereabouts
He'd find the numbers to resolve his doubts.

Do they see what I'm seeing? Gobs of ink
With daubs of bistre, ochre, puce and fawn
Beside some frantic scarlet: you might think
Those flowering apple-trees and cloud-filled dawns,
Those long-robed geishas, pearly, ruby, pink
Had no existence, never had been drawn:
And then a Nymphéas' embroidery
Asserts its movement irredeemably.

I think of Peter and I think of Pierre,
Some sixty years apart in eighty-one,
Wrangling most amiably, not just here –
'I don't see any bridge' but also on
The floor above, Peter inclined to jeer
At that sunset, at that 'Impression'.
I doubt if Monet pondered, had a clue
How that one word would question what men knew—
Or rather, what they saw. When Delacroix
Painted those liquid drops wherein the lake
And malachite lay hidden, à la fois
Visible and imperceptible, he'd break
No special taboo, nothing hors la loi:
A double generation it would take

To split the critics and the world apart—
There's no retidying that apple-cart.

I wish I had a grandchild here to show
The mobile colours of the air, to seize
The luminous unity—even though
I doubt she'd listen—grasp that harmonies
Even by way of discords here below
Are general, expound so that she sees
That Raphael's not Bosch nor plaster saint.
How can we know the painting from the paint?

Deux de la Vague 2011

Where has it gone, that army of ouvreuses
Who shoved you to your narrow creaking chair
And left complaining, short of twenty sous?
To-night you could drift off, sleep, unaware
In cushioned ease—and yet the memories
Come flooding back, insistent, hard to bear:
I don't eat cake, I'll skip the madeleine;
And trust skull-cinema to entertain.

Familiar images in black and white,
Inevitable endings: 'Jules et Jim',
'A bout de souffle'—the mood exactly right—
Truffaut whose life became a paradigm
In movies, Godard spoiling for a fight—
Those theorists of subjects fit to film:
A story Oscar told of the Wild West
'Don't shoot the pianist, he does his best.'

To wake alone in rue de Mexico
And hear loud chatter from the room next door;
'Why was 'North by Northwest' entitled so?'
Six voices argued, countered, wiped the floor.
Hitchcock meant thrillers and four hundred blows
An untranslateable bit of folklore:
That summer's education formed the heart
Of all I learned about the seventh art.

At first a pleasant process, osmotic,
La Dolce Vita where careless rapture
Gave way to Vitti fronting volcanic
Acres of desolation. L'aventure

Turned into that gloomy panegyric
Of urban Night and Fog, controlled despair
Exquisitely perceived, whose picture shrinks
To two sad lovers, humping on the links.

How many times we went to see Resnais'
Hiroshima—sleepy Nevers, that girl
Whose single mantra made the horror stay
As something human, comprehensible:
Those lovers too, like Keats's, fled away,
Leaving their ikons irreversible
And unrepeatable. The petrichor
Was showing something we'd not seen before

Whose transient beauty could be replayed
If not recaptured. Truffaut tried again
Insistently and there's a kind of thread
Between his films. 'La Nuit Americaine'
If not a swansong, marked a watershed—
A cinematic symbol whose refrain
Fused reel to music, improvised a tune
In making pictures like the last tycoon.

We stay to watch the credits; as they scroll
I think of English Empires—that stampede
To reach the corridor before the toll
Of drums. Another world, as we concede
With giggles as we leave. They played their roles
Without affection or with fratricide:
Aggressive, plangent, delicate, obscene.
They won no Oscars but they changed the screen.

Land of the Troubadours (Compleynt)

I have heard the innkeepers saying
'Six cents francs'
Very quickly—and then, expressively—
'Tout est compris.'
I have watched the traffic lights changing
In the proprietress's mind,
Hearing her say
'Seulement parce que vous êtes étudiant'
(Charging me extra).
I have heard the whine of motors
And their klaxons
Hooting at butterflies.
I have talked to the seedy curés
Who gave me a lift when their flock
(No doubt good Catholics) by-passed me.

I have seen this country of châteaux and valleys
Enlivened by posters
In three clashing colours—
Banners at Aultaforte—
And I have talked to several people
Who seemed to have no faith left in it.

I have been barked at by half the dogs in France
And seen off by three of them
As well as by various ladies
Who doubted the depth of my purse.
I have seen sunset over Aubeterre
Moonrise on Sarlat
And dawn in Chalais.
I have bought postcards, here and in Perigueux,
And peanuts in Ribéyrac,

Souvenirs in my haversack—
Crumpled paper and husks—
Tramcars in a cathedral cloister, mobile holiness
Recollected in tranquillity.

And damn it, you need a well-oiled engine to cover
    the area
Not just feet and fanaticism.

I have heard the Dordogne murmur
And the Dronne whisper
And the tourists repeating
'Ça c'est joli ça'
And the pedants propounding
'The language of hands which matters.'

And I have heard
The dulcet
Voice of the poet
Saying 'Merde.'

Limoges 1959

October Letter
—to Peter and Bar

The leaves are turning.
You imagine, I suppose,
In those half-formed imaginings
Centred on me, if one should speak my name,
Mediterranean azure, dusty roads,
Colours in gold and rose and pastel brightness,
Mountains, perhaps, with cypresses,
Landscapes by Perugino.

Two days ago it was dark
At five o'clock, and we sat
Planning our winter, while the cars passed
Plastered with starlike leaves,
In the faintly uneasy odour of autumn—
A familiar and welcome phenomenon—
Giving rise to only a fleeting qualm
For the flying, already forgotten, sun.

You will laugh at my nostalgia
But here too the heather is blooming.
The woods' charivaria,
Multicoloured, submarine shading
Of olive and scarlet and lincoln green,
Where the rain drips with the same note,
Is as familiar as reaching home
In the evening after a hard day,
And the moorhen's flight upriver -
A time or a thing to remember -
And say
It is like that in Yorkshire.
What is different is the uncertainty
Of thought in idleness.
There's no precise conviction
That 'this thing's to do'—
Harvest to finish in a rising gale,
Cows to be fed and milked,
Hens to be watered—
Only a suggestion
One would like to be able to express
And doesn't know to be worth expressing.

After the cobalt, hyaline days,
I sit here, quiet at nightfall,
And the leaves fall,

And the doves converse sleepily,
And I walk, as I would do at midnight,
Between the tracks of the railway, homewards,
Over the riverbridge where the moorhens sleep,
Through fields of moonlight, fallen
On quietly munching sheep,
Regarding inflexibly the point where the lines
Seem to meet in the darkness
And aiming for that
As if it were a distant star.

Aix-en-Provence 1961

Reading Proust in a punt near Grantchester

He isn't part of my syllabus and Father
Would call it typical bloody-mindedness though
My tutor is tolerant—maybe he'd rather
I followed my instincts on what I need to know

Like how muddy the Cam is here: not green nor deep -
Not even bordered by granges with solitary maids
Dwelling remote and unattainable, to peep
Behind curtain of privet or osier glades.

My thoughts are with Joanna, Meg and Rosemary
Instead of *The Allegory of Love* and Donne.
The happy years are those which are wasted if we
Accept wisdom comes through shameful incarnations.

My nenuphars float out towards the other bank
Beyond which lies a field of buttercups, golden,
Shining: the lilies waver, hesitate, break ranks
And then, across the current, slowly drift again.

Clearly the Vivonne in Normandy flows quicker,
Which makes it easier to speculate upon
Minnows in jam jars or those liquid prisoners
Pent in walls of glass which the Elizabethan

Sonneteers bang on about. What interests Proust
Once he's finished with the water's transparency
Is the lilies' regular pendulum—the roots
So fixed, the flowers condemned in perpetuity,

Which makes him think of Hell—not Ixion's wheel nor
Paolo and Francesca but of Dante and his
Fear of losing Virgil, whence he flits to decor
By Watteau so that you question his processes

Of thought. I see him sitting at the water's edge
Among the red and purple of the iris flames,
Counting the carp—unknown hereabouts though
                    the sedge
Opposite reminds me of bamboo and Needham,

Another one who made of remembrance an act
Of morality, high art—I'm doing the same
But less assuredly, spinning an artefact
Out of poem and place and dream, a kind of game

Which nobody wins for there isn't an answer -
To stop telling stories or manning the barricades
Is as impossible as to dessicate water
Or dissipate a fog by throwing hand-grenades.

Courances

for Jeanne-Marie and Annette

Most people have played games with water
And lose that particular childish obsession
In favour of order and cleanliness.

Using water to wash is a semi-civilised notion
Which must have occurred before anyone thought
Of hydraulics or Archimedes jumped out of his bath.

Before the cataract came into common usage
The play of fountain excited the rich and cultivated
In Rome, Persepolis and Xanadu.

Looking into a pool could be classed narcissistic
But reflection is a more than ambivalent pastime
When induced by octagonal tarns or rectangular lochs.

(Did Boileau and Rapin, for instance, know what
They were doing to drama when they set out to clarify
Aristotle in seventeenth-century France?)

At the same time Le Nôtre père cannot have dreamed
Of what he was starting in a landscape Stendhal called flat
With only a river and fourteen natural springs.

Whatever the consequences, what he did here
Seems effortless and even that statue from Marly
Is an irrelevance compared to the languid splashes of carp.

About two thousand years before he got busy
Eupalinos drove a thousand metre aqueduct
Through Samos with practical Greek precision—

A mega-construction problem solved by mechanics.
The only difference here is the lack of coercion
Though the course of the river seems to have changed completely.

However grand this canal and however precise
Its embankments, you cannot help wondering why
It lies where it does and where is the symmetry?

It has no practical purpose apart from indulging
A rich man's whim. 'Make me a garden where I may walk
At evening, without distraction from my friends' converse.'

Which meant that wherever the water went, it had
To be silently. If you follow the Rond de Moigny
Back to the woods, there is only a stone drain rill

Which ends at a miniature grimpen
With steadily throbbing teardrops that hardly seem
To know where they are going but keep on pulsating

Quietly, quietly. So you start to think about physics
And fluids and, sooner or later, you come to the Nappes
Where the deflux is noiseless but strong and you wonder,

You wonder why there are three and there isn't a torrent
And that's the beginning of wisdom. You can be here alone
Or surrounded by people but still you must marvel

How everything seamlessly wanders from vista
To vista and always with water behind. Le Nôtre
Might not have read Heraclitus but somebody must.

At Courances, if indeed everything flows, it does so
Hardly perceptibly and a walk in Elysium
Is accomplished with minimal fuss.

An Education 1954

In Memoriam: Philip Nash, Classical Scholar d.1968

It might have begun in Covent Garden: Tamino
Pursued by a monster which creaked and expired,
Like the production, which left me exultant, though
Worried about the dust. All I have are some snaps,
With half of them out of focus, in any old order,
And an exercise-book with two dozen pages
Of diary and place-names, untidily scrawled.

Crossing the Channel is not, even the first time,
Something to write home about, least of all
At night and arriving prior to dawn, complete
With packets of duty-free Senior Service.
Beyond the tree-lined autoroute stood tall stooks
Waiting for horse-drawn trailers: there wasn't a tractor
In sight as we found our way to the Bloedput
And breakfast, before we set off to explore on foot.
Rereading the route, I marvel at all our Virgil
Managed to compass: packed into an ancient
Wolseley, whose engine gave constant trouble, he drove
Through six countries with three callow youths and two tents
Each day for a month.
                        That first morning, the bell-tower
In Bruges wasn't open but statues of the Madonna
In street-corner niches, stepped gable-ends and poplars
Sprouting from brick-built spires, and boats on canals
We hadn't expected, gave scenes to record.
We ticked off Gand, Bruxelles, Namur: a list
Unlikely to evoke wonder: in fact, the unforgettable
Bits that day were the omelette and wine in a bistro
At Rochefort, just down the road from a campsite
By a river, where the lingua franca was Dutch.
More little photos chart nightstops in Luxembourg

And the Schwarzwald; a print of Strasbourg steeples;
A dinner of lager and bratwurst; a helping hand which
Adjusted the points as we crept up the Brenner.
The mountain taverna where we ate had a garage:
With no space to pitch our tents, we slept on its floor
And free-wheeled down to Bolzano, where the dynamo,
Belatedly, was replaced. We all have our memories
Though not always, alas, the faculty
To recall them but what is a memory if
Unrecalled?
        My diary says rainstorms and thunder
But all I remember is sunlight and sleeping
In vineyards with olive trees. First, on the shore
Of Lake Garda, a trattoria where we were introduced
To veal and chianti and then to Catullus
And his all-but island where we proceeded to swim.
I am not a bald head, nor have I forgotten my sins—
I could converse about the warmth of the water
And how the world is a holy place in which man
Is allowed to wander and contemplate carvings
Like those in San Zeno. From there we discovered
Another olive-strewn vineyard whose friendly padrone
Would have liked to invite us for dinner, had it not been
He was due at the opera, where we also contrived
To get in. I don't like masses of people but a mass
Of passionate cognoscenti waiting, intent on
Aida, in a sea of thirty thousand small candles,
Is something at odds with Mussolini or football
Or the sound of the Warsaw Concerto on scratchy
Seventy-eights.
        The assault on each of my senses
Continued in Venice and Padua, both within
Twenty-four hours but I don't need uneven paving-stones
To relive the delight our Virgil communicated
 At finding, in the Badia, a Filippo Lippi

Vision of Saint Bernard which forced me to look,
Or to picture the mazarine blue of the Scrovegni chapel.
We went back to our Veronese vineyard (more opera)
And then to Bologna for fleas and motocycletti: one hears
Horror stories about municipal campi but I guess
All our chance locations are inaccessible now.
The snapshot I cherish has two white oxen pulling
A plough, at evening on the slopes of Fiesole—
Our next port of call and another haven with olives—
Where we managed to stay for four consecutive nights.

My two large Folio tomes on The Art of Florence
Are consulted mainly for crosswords when I am stuck
Between knowing so little while knowing as much
As I do. I suppose we did in four days what1
An eighteenth-century noble would look at for months
But a lot of it stuck. For instance, about Fra Angelico—
Whose frescoes in cell after cell of the Convent
San Marco had kept us involved for hours and whose
Various Madonnas, those lapis-clad figures
With their respectful attendants in amber and vair
On a golden background, were a pictural précis
Of what the Renaissance in Italy was about—
We didn't connect with the fact that he came from Fiesole
When we toured San Domenico, unescorted
By Virgil, who'd left us to go to the Palio.
I don't know how much he cared about what we did
But I know we spent the day looking at pictures.
In the last part of the Divine Comedy there's a moment
When Dante is so interested in what he's discovering
That he forgets about Beatrice, the love of his life,
And she laughs: I think something like that was the plan
And for me it succeeded—that entirely beautiful Venus
Still lives in the Uffizi and I still measure
Masculine beauty by figures from San Lorenzo.
If I were to mythologise further as lucently

As memory will allow, it's that concert Overture
Leonora when the trumpet that came from a steep
On the other side of the Pitti reminded us
That the world is a holy place.
                                    I suppose
What we began to learn was discrimination
With tolerance: to appreciate that wearing shorts
In a duomo holding a mass was not de rigueur
Was an embarassing lesson and one we regretted,
Concurrently having an apprehension
That some places are holier than others and often
The sanctified ones are inclined to disseminate
A perceptibly squalid aura.
                                    What remains,
After Florence and some forgettable one-night stops
In Toscana, is an exhibition of buildings
And loci—a few recorded on postcards but many
Indelibly stamped on my mind—where I ask myself
Why I have never returned. I don't need to:
The towers of San Gimignano and Siena's Duomo
Compete with that tunnel-like gate at Volterra,
Deliberately on the skew from the road to catch
The attacker on his undefended side, and maybe
A thousand years older and seeming to lead,
As somebody said, to a Dantesque world.
Having absorbed already folklore of Galileo
We gave Pisa's Tower a cursory glance—
It was over-familiar and we wanted ice-cream.

We recrossed the Apennines, ending not with a bang
But an overnight train from Milano, coming back
To the pallid North in a British Rail diner
With a dawning perception there had to be something more
Than a limp slice of ham, two leaves and a lonely tomato
Or a late-night supper of baked beans on toast.

Semper eadem

Who was Mademoiselle
Enjoyed Madame
As, unashamed, she hung
Upon my arm.

When someone calls Madame
Mademoiselle
Her dignity demands
That she play hell.

Madame Mademoiselle
However, rows
Exactly as she did
Before her vows.

Place Names

Not far from Medina del Campo
There's a little village called
Madrigal de las Altas Torres
Whose claim to fame is that it was
The birthplace of Isabella of Castile.
Her claim to fame was that she
Provided the wherewithal for Columbus
To go looking for China.
He failed but the village with a name
Like a fanfare of trumpets
Remains, being undistinguished
Otherwise.

In the late nineteen-fifties it
Was still possible for hitchhikers,

Providing they looked fairly tidy,
To get picked up by lady drivers.
Coming out of Rochechouart
En route to Limoges I was told
By one of them as we passed
A signpost 'C'est Oradour' at which
I gave her a blank look. So she
Diverted to Oradour-sur-Glane
And told me its claim to infamy
Which remains.

The Auvergne, according to
General de Gaulle is that bit
Of France which nobody wants.
Maybe nobody told him
About La Chaise Dieu whose name
Suggests God might have chosen
His resting-place. Certainly
One of those Avignon popes
(Another one from the Corrèze)
Took a shine to it and picked
It for his mausoleum which
Is still there.

Nothing particular ever
Happened at Robin Hood's Bay
And neither Wesley nor Walmsley
Were actually born there.
If however you live there for
Thirty-odd years it seeps into
Your system: the line of the peak
Flows so naturally down and curves
In such a dramatic satisfying
Sweep that you disdain to go foreign,
Though it has nothing to do with
Robin Hood.

Ronas Voe

Sonnets for Sylvie about landscapes and solitude

Why should Gavin Douglas claim he saw them,
Palamedes birds, crouping in the sky?
Both place and season are impossible
(As first beginnings doublecross desire).
I see him at his casement hear anthems
Of white-front and pink-feet fading and I
Can feel an osmosis, intangible
Transmutation, dull the idea, tire
Into everyday love. Nowadays cranes
Don't fly in Scotland but the alphabet
Is hardly remarkable when goose skeins
Still straggle. From any old parapet
You can scan, peruse the mind's offerings:
After all, things only seem to be things.

After all, things only seem to be things
And Hamlet saw that cloud so mighty like
A whale, a camel or a what you will,
But you have to start somewhere. Start with A
Then, alpha, lambda and pi, rigid wings
Locked tight against the sky, pothook or pike
To copy, conquer, put into words and thrill
To the trumpet-tongued barnacle and grey;
Cry, if you like, with the Gabriel hounds
(Or tell court huntsmen that the king will ride).
To express the inexpressible sounds
A symbolic affair, something that pride
Or arrogance lead to a new estate,
An undiscovered country, desolate.

An undiscovered country, desolate
In the wild wet wind with the greylags' knell,
The khaki hills rip-moulded in the flood
(So difficult to say just what I mean)
Whatever is doubtful, dire, apostate,
Clings, crumbles on my tongue. Weeds in the swell
Pattern wings in the sky, words writ in blood
On the empyrean, ultramarine
Zone. Let me begin to spell and exult
Like a child learning. First I must falter
Through patter and nostrum, let the result
Surprise both of us. The hereinafter
Is brief and laborious, fearful, clear:
Your face in mine eye, mine in yours appears.

Your face in mine eye, mine in yours appears
Like symbols which were always there, patient,
Sapient, eta and eros, kappa
And caritas, not love but charity
Which suffereth long, is wise. You, my dear,
Know all about charity and sentiment,
A word I mistrust. If Virgil has a
Few blank spots like Dido or the swart sea,
His gravitas holds things together when
Palamedes birds start crouping. Acorns
May burgeon forty years on and open
New springs of emotion, feelings that mourn
Like Dido for something they find analogue:
The haunting goose-cry from a swathe of fog ....

The haunting goose-cry from a swathe of fog
Ought not to be alien, stranger-type;
Their migration follows the Yorkshire coast
And hunters hear it on high and depart
To habitual moorland fen and bog,
Places I know, where the plaintive sad pipe
Of Golden Plover, echoing like ghost
The Curlew's ecstatic bubble, is part
Of my childhood, like learning the archer
Who shot at a frog (clearly a nutcase)
Or speaking when spoken to, not before,
Which taught you to listen, find other ways
To establish your family place and
To say 'This is my true, my native land'.

To say 'This is my true, my native land'
Is something fewer of us can declare
As we disentangle genes which Darwin
Only guessed at. Runes and microliths still
Come to light after heather fires. Legends
Of giants compete with fossil of bear
And hyena. It's hard to imagine
How facts well-known to Pythagoras will
Vanish and only get resurrected
Two millenia later when someone
Bothers to think but then all has been said
And we come too late. 'What is my nation?'
Is only of any importance when
You try to explain to your grandchildren.

You try to explain to your grandchildren
How once, in Provence, a sub-prefect went
Outside to practise his oratory—
And bees buzzed in lavender, hoopoes bounced
Over thyme, frogs croaked in such unison—
That he stopped planning his lecture and bent
His mind to writing poems and stories
People might listen to. And he announced,
Perhaps, that this was his true vocation
And from henceforth this was to be his line
And if nobody read him now, someone
Might someday, somewhere. He had to resign
Himself to oblivion, be aware
One lonely place gives way to another.

One lonely place gives way to another—
A solitary hagg with three mallard
Patrolling a wind-shrivelled pine
Near Goathland transmutes to a Shetland tarn
With a raingoose lamenting a smother
Of snow on the wind—there's a Scottish word
For it in a Prologue (seven or nine)
With which Douglas adorned his translation,
A lonely task he did not hesitate
To abandon for a bishop's palace:
We don't know if he enjoyed high estate
But it was transient – quite soon he was
Cast like dross from some eternal smithy,
Wet in the mindless flood of Hell, Lethe.

Wet in the mindless flood of Hell, Lethe:
There are forgotten hamlets all over
Our Riding – one, Tranmire (Lake of the Cranes),
Has only three granges, a pool and, as
In the rest of the country, certainly
No cranes. There are peewit and harrier
And Old Castle Farm, which Domesday disdains
To note, though the map boasts a tumulus.
Tingon, on the south side of Ronas Voe
Has chapel ruins in rampant heather
And literally piles of stones. We know
Nothing about the people who lived there
And were dispossessed, any more than we
Understand fears we too will cease to be.

Understand fears we too will cease to be
And realise our own unimportance -
Familiar words from pulpit and lectern:
  'So to myself I said The dice are rolled,
   When all goes well, thank Virgil and not me,
   Write as I may with single diligence
   To recreate old wisdom and relearn
   The knowledge lost through ignorance, or sold
   In the market where none come to purchase
   Or flushed away in spasms of birthing pains ...'
We don't know where he died and his disgrace
Is unrecorded – and as for the cranes,
We still haven't answered the conundrum
Why should Gavin Douglas claim he saw them.

John Walker House

When the monasteries went, for a time
The economy faltered. Trade only picked up
As the seaways regained their ascendance,
The staithes were begun and the wreckers discouraged.

Hazards like storm surge, tide-rip and cloudburst
Are endemic for sailors; calculating risks
Is something they learn very early. Nobody knows
What the first owner did for his living
But a seaman like Walker can hardly have failed
To perceive the advantage of harbourside dwelling,
With wharfage at hand, a window to spy
On the market and the Meeting-house over the lane.

The takeover must have been gradual but wealth
Has a way of expressing itself in its buildings.
A modest house with a plaque according to Pevsner
(Who must never have seen the inside) was commodious,
Even stately, the panelling crafted with care
Like the bow-fronted door. No pictures or carpets
But all made to last like the tiles from Delft in the salon,
Long since disappeared.

       If the coal trade was bread
Then the alum was Yorkshire butter. Newcastle and London
Each had their own business connections
And then there were marts in the Baltic. Poldavy,
Cordage and spars came back to the roperies,
The seas around Greenland methodically cleared of whales
And soon the landholdings doubled and trebled.
Owning so much of Whitby compelled them to open a bank.
Keeping it in the family is all right as long as

There is one but the house lived on when the Walkers
Died out and might have been sold for a song. I suppose
It's a miracle no one destroyed it, not even the council,
Though doctors and nurses and reverends all
Left their mark.

You can still walk by without seeing
That James Cook lived for a while in the attic
And the shop next door is dealing in plastic ducks.

Love-letter for Jeanne-Marie

The Mortemart family had a particular
Way of talking—a series of languishing wails—
Instantly recognisable by courtiers
Who never knew whose turn it was to be mocked.

I can still hear your peals of amusement, your low-pitched
And throaty expressions—'C'est une honte,' 'C'est
Scandaleux,' or, with conviction but lacking
In venom 'Tu as tort.' Very often I had

But that didn't stop you from listening. Once,
Accidentally, we came to a church or a street
Called St Elizabeth de Hongrie, which made me recount
The story of bread and the roses. You laughed

'Oui, je m'en souviens.' Your telephone calls
For some reason, always began with 'Oui' and one wondered
Where they had started, like some of those peregrinations
Which often we have to beware of retreading.

At the Place de Furstenberg, for Delacroix,
You stayed outside, beneath the paulownias
And listened enchanted while the man with an organ
Of fifty-odd partly-filled glasses played Bach.

Another time, not far away, we discovered
A plaque overlooking a parklet, put up by a great
Great-uncle—that was the day when the St Sulpice
Curé got very worked up with the innocent tourists,

Followers of *The Da Vinci Code*, which I think
You read at one sitting—an awful addiction

Like 'Plus Belle la Vie' (for which everything stopped)
—Both difficult to connect to the scholar

Directing the drama who, when you asked me
To talk about Antony and I quoted a line
Of Pascal, said 'Attention! Cela continue …'
And recited the next four lines without recourse

To a text. Or the corridor outside your room
In the clinic with a clutch of nurses and interns
All agog to 'Waiting for Godot' within.
You could chat to the half-cut guys selling pot

On the steps of the metro Abbesses
Or anyone else in Montmartre (an inherited gift)
And go home to *Clarissa*. (Amazingly
It exists in translation). When I said Leavis

Preferred it to Proust, you fell back on Molière –
'Le pauvre homme,' you said, provoking momentary
Hysteria. Faut-il qu'il m'en souvienne
La joie: for which we say Thank you, remembering

That Madame de Montespan too had a génie
For listening—and maybe that's what we're missing
When we walk the remains of the St Martin towpath
And talk of the Hotel du Nord or le Père Lachaise

Where, unlike Rastignac, you would never say
'A nous deux maintenant' on the summit,
Preferring instead to give us and your city
A final glance of amusement mingled with love.

Spectator

Pourquoi espessit l'araignée sa toile en un endroit et relasche en un
autre? Se sert à cette heure de cette sorte de neud, tantost de celle-là,
si elle n'a et deliberation, et pensement, et conclusion?

(Why does the spider make her web denser in one place and slacker
in another, using this knot here and that knot there, if she cannot
reflect, think or reach conclusions?)

Montaigne: Apologie de Raimond Sebond

Long ago there were cricket matches when nothing seemed
To happen. You were content to sit on a concrete slab
In a seemingly somnolent crowd which awoke
To clap maiden overs and cheer the odd boundary.

Some of them of course were quite knowledgeable. They would
Cheer for a sketchy single and, if you asked, explain
That it was his ten thousandth first class run. It all
Resembled nothing so much as reading Montaigne

And that, at least, is still a civilised pleasure:
I can take the Latin quotations for maiden overs,
Whose worth becomes clear when I check the translation,
And the aperçus, single-liners which hit you for six.

Our well-being is only a state of not feeling uneasy
(On changing position because your left buttock's gone numb)
No reason can be established except by another reason
(Note: this was a time when the umpire's judgement was law).

One has to beware of regretting a golden age
Which never existed though what I remember
Is endless summer, whether spectating in Yorkshire
Or, about ten years later, walking in the Dordogne.

We must have passed less than a couple of miles away
From that sweet ancestral domain to which he retreated
To devote himself to freedom, calm and leisure -
No mention of essays—at the ripe old age of thirty-eight.

I should like to have seen the chateau with its towers—
One for his other half and one for his library—
Where you can still be reminded that two things are certain:
That nothing is certain and nothing's more wretched than man.

The knowledgeable reader will at this point remark
That this comes from Pliny the Elder—one advantage
Of Montaigne is that he cherry-picks from the classics
And saves you the trouble of having to read them yourself—

Which, when you come to think of it, is what Shakespeare
Did with Florio's translation: when Hamlet tells Claudius
A king may go a progress through the guts of a beggar,
That's Montaigne's imperial Caesar, eaten by tiny worms.

In the Oxford Book of Quotations, the only one from Tourneur
Is the usual dissertation about the skull
But you can't help suspecting that silkworm was the one
Which metamorphosed in Raymond Sebond's Apology

Anymore than you can't help admiring those calm
Meditations on death: if he did indeed flee
From the plague in Bordeaux, it's a human reaction:
His immense erudition had borders of commonsense.

To return to our purpose: the laws of cricket,
It used to be said, could be used to reinvent,
If necessary, the British Constitution,
Still largely unwritten and based on a sense of fair play,

Which is what makes Montaigne familiar:
You can't imagine him stating, like one famous
French intellectual, that he wasn't good at stupidity,
Because of that tentative 'After all, what do I know?'

Homage to Giono
North West Foxe, etcetera
(2012)

Homage to Giono

1. Where Autumn Starts

I suppose you know when autumn arrives,
    Where autumn starts?
You must count two hundred and thirty-five
    Paces apart
From the tree marked three one two. I've counted
    Them exactly—
It all depends if you have visited
    The col Menet.

The lac du Lauzon, do you know the track?
    Just at the place
It crosses the chamois fell, there's a crack
    Between two faces
Of steep rockfall which brings you directly
    Under the west
Slope of Ferrand. Here the geology
    Detains, arrests—

It's perfectly telluric, mineral land:
    Gneiss, porphyry,
Sandstone, decaying schist, serpentine and
    The Lus aiguilles,
The horizons ringed: hound's teeth, incisors,
    Molars, canines.
You can go left to Ferrand, visitor
    To things alpine,

Or venture right, across the diatoms.
    Eventually,
In a bowl like earthenware, you will come
    To a spinney,

Very high, perhaps two hundred trees. Mark
    On the north face
An ash with three one two, red in the bark,
    And you must trace

Exactly two hundred and thirty-five
    Paces apart
To the other ash where autumn arrives,
    When autumn starts.
It's instantaneous. Was there, maybe,
    Last night, while you
Were making soup, an order silently
    Sent down below?

This morning you awake to find the tree
    Has a golden
Yellow crest on its head. Drink your coffee
    And you will then
Find your crest transformed into a helmet
    Of rare feathers—
Pinks and greys and endless shades of russet
    Foliature.

Then come embellishments, the epaulettes,
    Decorations
Descending with cuirasses and breastplates
    All in motion,
In a gleaming world of vermilion
    And silver copes,
Pennons and frills and furbelows as worn
    By warring popes.

Three one two is not standing still either
    But he favours

More priestly garments—cassocks the colour
       Of honey or
Bishop's frocks with emblazoned stoles. Larches
       Rapidly don
Cowls and raiment of marmot skin. Maples
       Quickly put on

Red spats, zouave trousers, executioner's
       Capes and a hat
For a Borgia. You must have time for
       Absorbing that
Though meadow saffrons blue the chamois field
       As you return
From Ferrand, and a gaudy sunset yields
       An afterburn:

That haycock which you passed two days ago
       Has turned deep bronze—
Around it you can count, on sentry go,
       The Indians,
The blood-hungry Aztecs, panners of gold,
       Ochre miners,
Popes and cardinals, archbishops and old
       Knight foresters.

Imagine then tiaras, bonnets, helms,
       Costumes of vair
And painted cloths, embroidered folds. The elm,
       Aspen, elder,
Birch, oak, ash, beech, maple and sycamore
       —Lovats and mints—
Against the green-black of the conifers
       Exalt their tint . . .

          (*Un roi sans divertissement*)

2. Two Sonnets to the Beech

In all the woods this is the nonpareil:
We know it has no equal in the land—
No smoother bark, no statelier array,
No shape more balanced nor with more command—
Apollo of all beeches. The highway
Encompasses a hairpin where it stands
Overflowing with wings—they float like spray—
Bee swarms, unkindnesses of ravens and
Watches of nightingales—the tree breathes flies,
Smokes hornet and warbler, juggles with balls
Of multi-coloured chaffinch, butterfly
And wren that flit across the rainbow falls.
The forest ranged around the mountain flanks
Looks on in silence at the teeming ranks:

Then, in the autumn, views the long crimson
Tendrils, the thousand arms enlaced with green
Serpents, the hundred thousand leaves, golden,
Glinting with feathered tufts, aureolin,
Beribboned with birds. Or, when it listens,
Hears the crackle and the crepitating:
You cannot call it a tree. Its motion
Is dancelike, supernatural, spinning
Around itself, entwined in golden veils
And only maintained by prodigious roots
Or miraculous speed (like those angels
In countless armies wearing needle boots).
The forest, in its vast amphitheatre,
Gazes in awe, moves not an iota.

(*Un roi sans divertissement*)

3. Wolf Hunt

It is strange how though we all knew it was going
To happen—in a country such as ours
You cannot allow a wolf to slaughter twelve sheep
And make off with the thirteenth without reprisal—

Nevertheless we were taken aback to be
Summoned to school one evening. To be cheek by jowl
With childhood friends being given our instructions
—Very precise ones—carried us back to schooldays

And prepared us absorb the commander's plan:
Its meticulous detail impressed us as much
As the dozen horn-players summoned for the meet,
With the public prosecutor and retinue

All dressed up for the following day—a Sunday.
Then, lacking liturgy, the ceremonial
And solemn music established the feeling of awe
From the moment we started our battues at dawn.

Far off, the bleating of an adenoidal calf
Set off our rattles and encouraged our own horn
To give notice of our involvement, while away
On our other flank the forest calm was shattered.

Would you believe we curveted like stallions
Hearing trumpets? We went forward as if ready
To tear the wolf with our teeth, eyeing the bushes
Lest from one should spring the gaping red-black muzzle.

We were eyeing each other too, with amazement,
And realising the famous prosecutor,

Who told us to beware of truth because it was
True for everybody, was clearly not stupid.

We continued to follow instructions blindly,
Mainly in silence. The Chalamont outreaches
Are thickly wooded and it was all very well
To say that we would direct our prey with music:

We still had to stick to our patch. Wolves are malign
And the one we were after might very well say
To himself, 'If they think their noise will frighten me
In that direction, I'll take the opposite one'.

We went on thinking, plodding, swinging our rattles
Up till midday, hearing, from time to time, the calf
Sneezing questions —'Are you all right? Is everything
Going to plan?' Our horn reassured him (and us)—

'We are on time but we have seen nothing. All is well'.
We had a bite to eat and renewed our advance
Through the undergrowth and the fearfilled empty woods
As late winter afternoon light began to fade.

We began to see things, we had twenty false scares,
The denser thickets seemed to flicker together
Before our weary eyes, so that when it happened
What we saw was not at all what we expected:

A movement rather like a sidestep, slipping by
Unnoticed as an overloaded branch drops snow,
So we ploughed on till we came up to the debris,
Where the tracks suddenly began to worry us

Though we had no sight of the beast. Our horn sounded
The 'vue' as we read the signs of a sidewards leap

Leaving bare black limbs agonising on the white,
A splendid 'vue' producing a complete silence.

It was broken when the calf turned into a bull
And bugled commands for groups to converge on us
As we trudged into the heart of the Chalamont,
Which wasn't that easy and still held surprises.

We knew we would end up facing a gaunt stone cliff
And we knew what the spoor we had seen denoted—
An animal which, all day, had been subjected
To a weird brouhaha of horncalls and rattles.

It might not, we thought, be in the best of tempers
—If it was still a wolf. I pictured a giant
Ear, in which all our music had turned to venom,
Which was not wolf material. The ear was like

A funnel mouth, stuffed with the tails of a thousand
Snakes as long as your arm and it was in these snakes
That the venom had clotted, like black-pudding blood.
This I expected to find in the Chalamont

But it was slow to appear and we had trouble
Keeping in line. Then, as night fell, confusion reigned
For a moment, until we realised our prey
Was trapped at a bottle-end with us as the cork.

The horncalls continued, our own excited ones
Calmed by the commander's and the reality
Of lines of torches advancing from every side
And, eventually, no more than ten yards apart.

The commander took up his place in the centre,
Allowing the dogmaster to release his charge

Which disappeared into the darkness, silently.
And silently, red in the torchlight, we marched on.

There were the tracks, very obvious, tossed about
And turbulent, as many as we might require.
It was a peculiar saraband which he
Had performed, more silently than we could manage

Because of our torches which gave a rustling sound
Like coming and going of birds above our heads
—Doves, maybe, roosting; coming from a bigger Ark
Than the first, expending a flight of wood pigeon.

The spoor led on, showed no sign of anxiety,
And then we were clear of the trees on a bare floor
At the foot of the wall. The wolf awaited us,
Blinking in torchlight, the mastiff dead at his feet.

So things had been happening during the silence
We knew nothing about. What we saw was our chief
Who walked three or four paces forward, extending
His arms to restrain us. The wolf laid his ears back

And they faced each other, maybe five yards apart,
With the dog's blood staining the snow in between them:
Like us, the wolf seemed part of a dream as our chief
Raised his rifle and pumped two bullets into his heart.

(*Un roi sans divertissement*)

4. Spring

Disorder established a bridgehead
As conifers raised clouds of poldavy
And glades steamed up embers half-extinguished,
Smoking through deciduous canopies—
Imagine fires from Indian tepees
Or nomads travelling in vast number—
Their trembling shafts marking the delivery
Of Spring, awoken from winter slumber
And now determined to clean out last year's lumber.

The bridgehead expanded gradually;
Expectant clouds adopted brooding dark
And heavy forest odours—patently
Humus but with a memory of bark
And new grass, a hollow combe's selvage mark.
Unseen wells bubbled muffled carmagnoles
Stirring up pasture velvetly, while stark
Tall pines creaked like those bare despairing poles
Of clippers racing to antipodean goals.

Then a black Boreas came from the east
Bearing more confusion and endless squalls.
Clouds in the valleys heaved like rising yeast,
Then freed themselves to bounce as rubber balls
Across the sky—and great grey waterfalls
Hid every mountain and forest from sight.
Thin streaks of rain hung on the gale in shawls
Like hair from a goat's belly. Overnight
The wind sang in the woods, then went out like a light.

Then came the sun—a sun in three dense shades
Of red more vibrant than fox pelt, so warm
And thick that noises were extinguished,
Movement stopped, time out of war. The calm
Was momentary: the north wind rearmed.
A thousand silver flames lit leafless trees
And drops of shining water made a balm
For new buds burgeoning. Momently
There rose mixed odours of sap and fresh energy.

Even while standing water was seeping
Away, the fresh assault roared fiercely through
As breeze turned gale, rain and sun bestriding
The land in black stains with leis of rainbow.
Clouds rumbled on deep valleys, jerked as though
Electrocuted: their huge bubbles popped
Lightning. Thunder, dramatically slow,
Echoed down village streets as floods outslopped
Cellars. And then, amazingly, again it stopped.

More clouds began their accumulation
Slowly on the horizon; dapple grey
Acres of foliage and dark caverns,
Winding staircases climbing to displays
Of azure, cobalt, jacinth, in the rays
Cast by a sun growing in confidence,
Assuming more natural hues each day,
Its far-off turbulent incandescence
Warming the earth in riotous recrudescence.

With it, the fauna. The furred, the feathered,
Smooth-skinned, cold-blooded, warm, earth-diggers, wood-
Peckers, swimmers, runners and gliders, said
To themselves 'Swim, run, fly'—just as they should
At this season. More urgently, the blood
Began its questioning, its pursuing,
Through golden lattices and gilded floods
Of twilight, the schmaltzy paths of feeling:
Lovecalls beside the swollen river's thundering.

Glaciers thawed to thin little slivers
Snaking between rock striations; cascades
Grumbled down mountains, streams became rivers
With flotsam of stone and timber, foam sprayed
Treetop height. Stripped agonised branches played
Pavanes of slow despair as they were borne
Unresisting on a sea now so broad
It seemed unmoving, and only forlorn
White horses marked afar the constant torrent's bourn.

The escarpments whence it emerged were
Sheer, ivy-hung, clematis-wrapped, seething
With gossiping crossbills, warblers, waders,
Crows and nightingales calling, repeating
Questions: Where's the thaw? Are the floods waning?
Where are our mudflats, worms, water-boatmen,
Greasy brown roe and osiers smelling
So strong you can't breathe? And fat ptarmigan
Shoved rudely in: Hotch up, hotch up again! Again . . .

You can hardly say Spring had established
Itself because the confusion remained
But it was warmer. Dog foxes screamed. Fish
Were jumping. Tips of turtle-dove wings stained
The sky and cranes, outlined against it, planed

Northwards. Weasels mewed and otters, shining
And smooth, flowed lambently. A wolf complained.
Swifts ripped open veils of midges dancing,
Droning adieux to clouds which were sailing, sailing . . .

(*Le Chant du Monde*)

5. The Hussar on the Roof

(i) 'Vous avez, donc, habité Aix?'
'J'y ai séjourné pendant deux ans'
(p. 597)

('You have lived in Aix, then?'
'I lived there for two years)

Like Angelo, I lived there for two years at what,
I imagine, must have been about the same age,
Though roughly a century later. It's not easy to say
Which outbreak of cholera morbus Giono
Had in mind but the historical background to Angelo's
Excursions on rooftops in Manosque seems to point
To the Second Empire. (There's a scholarly 'notice'
In the Pléiade edition which states that Angelo
Would have been fifty in nineteen hundred – which
Makes no sense at all in this particular story,
A novel I only read towards the end of our stay
Not stopping for all the strange words I couldn't translate.)
By then we had walked many miles over burnt-out forest
And our one year old son could distinguish between
Lavender and thyme. We spent a year in the Arab quarter
Eking out a penurious existence
While having a ball; then we moved outside the city
And lived alfresco in an old pavillon de chasse

Where we slept in a leaky disused winepress
Of which Pauline and Angelo might have approved.

(ii)'Il n'eut de difficulté qu'à Aix qu'il fut obligé de
deborder à droite par Palette et jusqu'au pied
de Sainte Victoire.' (pp: 571-2)

(The only place where he had had difficulty was
at Aix where he had been forced to make a detour
to the right through Palette round the foot of the
Sainte Victoire.)

He (the clarinettist from the Marseille opera) went on
To describe how the bodies strewn along that pretty road
Seemed odourless, apart from the sarriette and thyme
In which they lay, always in noble attitudes, because
They had died with great vistas before them.
(It was here that the legions of Marius, at least
Two thousand years earlier, slaughtered a teeming mass
Of Teutonic barbarians, and here that Cezanne,
In quieter times, made la Sainte Victoire archetypal).
How lucky we were to be welcomed in Aline's villa
Beside the route de Palette: our own difficulty
In Aix was to find some dwelling we could afford
As the North African exodus had raised all rents.
Perhaps we were also lucky to be too innocent
To notice the tensions under society's façade
Or even to be aware we were being looked after
By a conspiracy of loving relations and friends.
It was Edwina who broke us in to horses
And show-jumping, and with her that we got to know Var
And the lower Alps (including Manosque). Perhaps
It was Angelo's absolute care for his horses,
With Giono's preoccupation with landscapes

We had just found, which combined to hold both of us
enthralled.

(iii) 'J'appelle ces moments-là des moments difficiles.'
(p. 358)

(These are the times which I would call difficult moments.)

What was worrying Angelo at that moment
Was the sight of a little girl in a frilly dress
Mincing delicately down the deserted street
Between plague-stricken houses, paying no heed
To a deep contralto voice calling out Holy Mary
Three desperate times. What worried me, late at night
In the rue du Puits Neuf, were the sounds from across
The roof where the tenant had a habit of beating
His wife—which was hardly what we associated
With Provençal custom. (There again, as Angelo
Reflected, Romeo and Francesca da Rimini
Both came to violent ends.) More happily, I recall
The showers, which seemed to occur exactly
At seven each morning (the municipal dustcart),
The fountain's splash at the end of the street
And the unforgettable coffee smell from the torrefaction
Across the way. The only desperate cries
Were those of the postman, too lazy to climb the stairs,
And the beggar lady who sang until someone paid her to stop.

(iv) 'Dans ces terres hautes, les rossignels nichaient tard. Angelo en entendit de très nombreux qui s'appelaient d'un bosquet à l'autre … Il se souvint que ces oiseaux étaient carnassiers.'

(pp: 294-5)

'In those high altitudes, the nightingales roosted late. Angelo heard many of them calling from one copse to another … He remembered that these birds were carnivorous.'

Some of Giono's ornithology seems as dodgy
As his recipes. Nightingales are certainly
Insectivorous but that doesn't make them flesh-eaters,
Though he is right about their wakefulness. It was bedlam
On early May mornings by the canal Zola
As nightingales competed with frogs in crescendos
Of passion, though I never threw anything at them.
While on the subject, Keats said he was half in love with death
(The emphasis is on 'half'). I don't think Angelo
Or I would have even considered the matter,
Being both determined to live our lives as intensely
As possible and, without being sentimental,
It was the intensity of the experience of which
I wrote: I have heard the nightingales singing
Each deep night, in May in Provence; and stopped,
Not because, like Angelo in the last line of the book,
I was 'au comble de bonheur' but because
That said it all. The happiness Keats wrote about
Came to a conclusion both with an expression
Of the experience and of his sense of completion,
The latter, one which Angelo had reason to share
Because of his singular triumph—that lonely battle
For Pauline's life.

        I can't make associations
With anything so dramatic during our life
In the Midi and I have forgotten some difficult moments.
But after fifty-odd years I look back on that landscape
Of thyme-clad garrigue and what Keats called
Provençal song and sunburnt mirth, and I'm grateful.

                        (*Le Hussar sur le Toit*)

North West Foxe

A Poem with Notes

In the back alleys off Church Street, on the East side
Of Whitby, you can still find the odd Tudor house
Where Foxe might have dwelt, but it's pure speculation.
His only monument is what he wrote himself.

The DNB biography, very briefly,
Concludes that he 'died neglected' which is, perhaps,
DNB-speak for 'chose to retire to Whitby'.
Nevertheless it is known that Phineas Pett,

The King's Shipwright, in early sixteen thirty-five,
Thought it worth his while to make the ride from Scarborough
—Twenty miles over rough moorland tracks—in order
To sound the North Riding Admiralty Marshal

About building ships on the cheap in the North East.
'Our Yorkshire proverb: 'Plain dealing is a jewel,'
Pett was told. Getting the message, he persuaded
His host to give him a true account of his voyage …

> If I am but a North country coaster,
> Brought up in the business of Whitby cats,
> Then I would make reply to my doubters
> They have but to look at the map, and that
> God's mercy is over all his creatures
> Including Master Urine and his mate.
> The secrets of crossing the Atlantic
> I learnt, but not the sense of their ethic.

What did they know of Frobisher and Hall
Or the disappearance of the Hudsons?
Of John Davis, if they knew aught at all,
'Twould be his voyage in the Southern Ocean
And his death in Jakarta. At his call
I would have sailed to share that elation
—Discovering an uninhabited
Country—where your feet are the first to tread.

I hoped to have sailed with Knight, as First Mate,
But I was too green, was forced to abide
My hour, though I had passed Gibraltar Strait
And traversed the Baltic. With care, I plied
My trade and continued to navigate
Through unknown seas in charts by my fireside.
When at last the chance was there for taking
I knew exactly where I was going.

What I did not allow for was the lack
Of ambition and imagination
In my lieutenants. I was thrown aback
By their failure to follow instructions
But yet we managed, despite them, to pack
Aboard all the spare gear and provision
For twenty-two crew over eighteen months.
I dipped my flag at Whitby, heading North.

If aught was amiss it was the shallop.
I regret not to have put the Master
And his mate ashore when we made a stop
In Kirkwall but how was I to know their
Replacements might not be worse? In one hop
Of twenty-eight days, the Charles crossed over
To the furious outfall, entering
The ice at Cape Chudleigh with clear sailing.

73

We could have made faster progress but for
The growls of the Master's mate, which caused me
To stand to the West when the North was clear
—He liked to shelter in an iceberg's lee
And reefed for any slight change in weather.
Beset among the western islands, we
Beheld the sun kiss Thetis in our sight
Five degrees west from north—the frost was white …

It may be that it is worth making the comment
At this point that the narrative speaks tarpaulin
—Seventeenth-century tarpaulin—and that Foxe
Had enough education for classical tags

As well as a mass of sailing directions,
With thinly disguised contempt for his officers
And self-confidence in all his preparations
Which contrast with an abiding sense of wonder.

   —The frost was white and prevented the pitch
From melting on even the sunward bow
When we made landfall at Cape Digges, which
Appeared but momently beyond our prow
In giant flocks of sea pigeon. We switched
Course to Hudson and Button, used the Plough
To sail on by night and lost our cutwater,
Which gave me cause to bless our carpenter

Before Master Pisspot had time even
To open his mouth. We interthreaded
Nottingham, Roe's Welcome and Southampton,
Islands earlier so designated
To record the enterprise and vision
Of these advancers. We navigated
Around the great bay – if I remember

Many events 'tis in the wrong order.

There came under the sheeting of our head
A Sea Unicorn, whose like we never
Had beheld. About four yards he measured,
His sides being spotted as a panther
But with milk-white belly. The watch declared
His form like to a mackerel but lobster-
Shaped his head whereout the forepart there grew
His twined horn six foot and black in hue.

A school of twenty followed him that night—
The watch below were moved to come on deck
For all the sea was full of whales: some white
And small and some leviathans whose wake
Rocked us. We kept our cold lodging, lay tight
And fast, the while the Master called for sack
And ate and was content to roll and sway
Southward as all the summer ebbed away.

When we chanced upon a herd of sea horse
I dare not stop until we were beyond
Cary Swan's Nest. In a black sea, our course
Was shifting, in thick fog. We had to stand
Behind another berg whereon were bears
Which we pursued, killing the one harpooned
And making oil, with meat that had a taste
Like beef when boiled but rank and sour when roast.

North in the firmament after four days
There came pettidancers (henbanes, as some
Do call them): that spectacle did amaze
Us and we feared it did foretell maelstrom
In the element—hues of chrysoprase,
Viridian, were streaked with cadmium

As they faded and left us to wonder
While starting to beat down the western shore.

I warned my sailors that the Indians
Were not to be abused howsoever
They might behave: also that the German
Ocean, despite its perils, was smaller
Than Hudson's Bay. With clear skies, we came on
Great store of fish and made an endeavour
To rig the skiff, discovering on land
Stone mounds like haycocks scattered in the sand …

Foxe makes me think of Cook, who also learnt his trade
In Whitby and was troubled by bad lieutenants,
Specifically on his last fatal voyage.
I think of his rule about the prime importance

Of friendship with native peoples, which has been used
As a proof of his forward-thinking and being
Ahead of his time. And then remember that Foxe
Was making his journey in sixteen thirty-one.

—Scattered in the sand, the mounds had been raised
And abandoned. The nomads' sepulchre
Yielded us firewood but we respected
The corpses, wrapped in their deerskins. There were,
All about them, arrows of ironwood,
Yew harpoons and longbows shaped from cedar.
Some arrows had copper and iron heads
Which must have come from European trade

Yet I do not recall such bartering
From my reading of Baffin and Button.
We met, of these Indians, none living,
Though a colony of geese we fell on,
In size as our Stubble birds but having

Black throats and white bellies, made a foison
Of fresh meat to feast on. In mid-August
We beached again, upon the southern coast.

By then I knew we needed scurvy grass
For I had seen the signs and commanded
The Master to get ready his pinnace.
It took him over an hour and I asked
How he would fare at night in a bourrasque
Or shipwreck? Thank God, they never happened.
They brought back grass whose juices I had ground
And then mixed with the morning strong beer round.

When I recall things, I'm not always able
To separate the reality from
What I would like to relate, the fable
Instead of the truth. In the end, the sum
Of our voyage was that navigable
Sea channels were not in that periplum.
There must have been nomads who were aware
Of this but, after all, why should they care?

When we met Captain James it was autumn.
I could tell him of Port Nelson and how
We had claimed its hinterland, a kingdom
Of gaunt wastes, of beasts of prey and wildfowl
Which we called New Yorkshire, should any come,
Though what could be their motive? It was now
That he advised me to overwinter—
His own intent – I left it for later.

He feasted us well and talked learnedly
Of navigation, refusing to dip
His flag because, he explained to us, he
Carried mail from the King to his worship

The Emperor of Japan. 'Certainly',
Quoth I. 'This may be the law of seamanship
But you are out of the way to Japan'.
I feared for him for he was no seaman.

We left him to follow his fantasies
A tale of avoidable misfortune
Which glorified his own incompetence,
Heading North with cares enough of our own.
Though we made swift passage, I knew our lease
Of summer was finished and very soon,
With scurvy again off Cape Dorchester,
I had but bleak choice by late September.

We lacked not for food as there were sea horse
In store on the islands, yet were our sides
And brine-tubs frozen and the snow got worse,
Lying thick each morn. If we chose to bide
It was freeze to death or seek for harbour.
In the end, it was easy to decide
Not to hazard the loss of our new knowledge
And my seamen's lives but risk the passage.

I named the point Foxe his Farthest before
Setting course for home—a command with which
The Master was for once pleased to concur.
He rose from his sickbed and did beseech
More sack, which gave me a chance to order
Extra course of sail. They brought us to reach
The Downs, glory to God, on All Saints' Night
With all the crew alive and all gear right.

Of course, there was nobody at the quay—
How could there have been? The best part by far
Of a journey is travelling and we,

In any case, weren't due back for a year.
It was a silent pay-off, thankfully.
I had no words for my master bugbear
Nor he for me, making haste to depart:
I kept my counsel though it wrung my heart.

You can set out three reasons why Foxe's voyage
Lacked popular acclaim: he took so little time
To do what he had to do, nothing went wrong and
The news he brought back nobody wanted to hear.

Beasts of Tonfanau

Our photographs on inaccessible
Beaches two hundred miles apart, with a
Fifty year gap, are recognisably
Us, we tell ourselves: the phenomena
Which confuse are the altered sceneries.
The mole where we fished at Port Mulgrave scaur
Disappeared in a howling north-easter—
The footpath now a playground for climbers.

The roads to Tonfanau seem to wind more
Inexplicably so I hardly knew
We'd arrived—at least there's a road. (Aber
Junction, down the line, is lost in bayou
Of mud, bulrushes and standing water).
On a ruined concrete road where reeds grew,
Unsure, we drifted over the railtrack
Exploring through ghost Bofors and seawrack.

The three scavenged shingle while I surveyed
A site I'd shared with fifteen hundred men,

Calling up troops who refused to parade,
Through guarded gates which were always open,
Now locked. Old hangars and stands of pine made
Ground-level screens and above, what had then
Been drill-squares, spider-barracks and mess-halls,
Were green pastures bounded by dry stone-walls.

I don't know who discovered the totem—
A sea-white fistful of roots laid claim to
By Elizabeth, while I ignored them,
Trying to capture some dying bellow
Of bombardier or clash with RSM,
While carloads of tourists proceeded to
Follow their own arcadian fancies,
Including eight miles round the estuary.

That's what we did for want of amusement
In an 'Is that all?' mood. No catharsis
Still less a déjà vu: my absolvement
Was gradual, as if by osmosis,
Though Elizabeth sent me a present –
A triptych 'Beasts from Tonfanau' which is
On my wall—gargoyles with satisfied leers—
Some kind of a sop to Mnemosyne?

Return Visit: Apologia
for Peter Scupham

Nothing stays put, not even the Cam. If Jamshyd
Did indeed drink rather too deep when liberty
Of access was tightly controlled, it might be said
That now the lion and the lizard wander free
And equipped with video cameras, despite
The more limited periods when the college
Is open to visitors, though legitimate
Tenants come and go at all hours. The privilege
Of attending another public school could be
Somewhat unappetising to a twenty-one
Year-old gunner—and the change, unfortunately,
Came just too late for me—Larkin's phenomenon.

I suppose what got me through that awful first year
Were the strange viands for the imagination:
Allegorical roses, misericord leer
Of goat-foot satyr and hermaphroditic faun
Apeeping as I punted beerily upstream.
Some friends who lasted and a tutor (who did not)
Made the second year bearable. Even in dream
I recall it with an aggrieved feeling of What
Did I miss (apart from inedible dinners)?
My third-year love, who has also lasted, altered
My timetable and way of looking at pictures
And shifted my focus to a different world.

I don't know when Piaf first sang her signature
Tune but, later, remember an aged Macmillan
Outfacing some American with his 'Never
Waste time on vain regrets as a politician'—
Which is why return visits to Cambridge are few

And short-stay. My osmotic re-education
In three years across the Channel gave me a new
Perspective from which to approach a vocation:
I fell into teaching willy nilly as prams
Piled up in our Yorkshire hall—at least, now we know
Which parts we play in the furniture. And the Cam,
As Heraclitus observed, continues to flow.

Sonnet 5

A child cries for the unattainable
Toy or moon that is somebody's plaything
In this block of experience, but not
His own. And he rages and kicks at stones
That impede him, because they are stable
And last night he didn't sleep well. Dreaming,
Perhaps, of a moment of movement out
And across and beyond yonder, and none

Of us know, or shall ever, deception
Of this magnitude. As great symphonies
Blare parabolically frustration,
The sun has dark places the child foresees
And avoids by instinct, but where we are
Meantime, the sun is only a small star.

Latin Lesson

In John Adamson's class, right from the start,
We sat in alphabetical order
Which meant, being a double u, my part
In the translation of Virgil bordered
On insignificance. I was the last
To be called but, amazingly, last night
While I was vainly trying to forecast
My chunk of text, there was this girl (Miss Wright)
Beside me, seeming to know not only
All about Orpheus and the underworld
But also the propagation of bees.
Being aware that my arm encircled
Her waist, she raised a quizzical eyebrow,
Continuing silently to translate.
It could not last and John came to see how
The trick was being performed but too late.
He must have been as frustrated as I
For I woke not remembering at all
What she looked like but for once at least I
Had had a dream worth trying to recall.

Sonnet for the English Faculty in the University of Aix/Marseille 1962

Dear Bill,
Hamlet's still selling, you'll be pleased to hear,
And blood and thunder, lechery and vice
Are at a premium, though comedy's
Inclined to date. That clown, in whom your trust
Was absolute, for whom you sketched the mere
Outlines—well, he died, since when we excise
The patchy bits and say they're forgeries
'Blurring the vision of your genius'.
And sometimes, something lacks in atmosphere—
Too much of Matthew's sweetness to permit
The lumpen proletariat to jeer
But thrills the intellectual élite.
    How would you write a comedy to-day
    To make both bourgeois and the workers pay?

Headmaster's Villanelle

A would-be classics teacher has no Greek
(How does one explicate Tereu, Jug Jug?)
Our handyman reports another leak.

Another term, another staffroom clique,
(I'd like to liquidate those Fifth form thugs)
A would-be classics teacher has no Greek.

Computerman complains there's not a squeak
(They're overloading the electric plugs)
Our handyman reports another leak.

I don't think the French miss will last a week
(We need another crate of plates and mugs)
A would-be classics teacher has no Greek.

Why does that Matron think a good physique's
An antidote to epidemic bugs?
Our handyman reports another leak.

Beyond the stables there's a dreadful reek
I wonder if the Sixth are into drugs?
A would-be classics teacher has no Greek
Our handyman reports another leak.

Poem for St George's Day 2012

The last time I felt patriotic must have been
Thirty years ago when we still had carriers
Equipped with aeroplanes. The one I was watching
Was sailing to fight for the last bit of Empire

At the other end of the world. My friend Arthur,
Our local builder, who had been there for some time
In the Second World War, informed me that it was
'Very like Orkney but much much further away'.

'No bloody trains, no bloody bus, nobody cares
For bloody us', quoth he when I asked what he meant.
At the time I was far too busy to ponder
The rights and wrongs of the matter. That came later,

When I accidently discovered James Cook
Had been responsible for naming South Georgia
(In seventeen seventy-five), which led me on
To when the Falklands were also untenanted.

It seems that in fifteen ninety-two they were found
By John Davis, who didn't bother to name them.
That was left to Richard Hawkins in ninety-four,
Who called them his 'maiden land' and went on his way—

Which seems to have been the norm for Las Malvinas
For the next couple of hundred years. They have been
Settled by all the usual Empire-builders,
The last lot arriving in the eighteen thirties.

And there they are still, another embarrassment
Like Gibraltar and very difficult to feel
Patriotic about, especially when you
Have to associate with the buffoons and rogues

Who flaunt the flag for entirely personal gains
And wish, like Eldon, for Chaos to be restored.
Coleridge realised the problem roundabout
The time when Boney was threatening to invade.

A plot whereon the numbers cannot try the cause
Suddenly endears itself when it happens to be
Your own. Which is why this particular Anglo-
Celt might feel bound to fight his little scrap of land.

Vichy

for Pierre François

Crenellated tinsel
Hung upon cotton
Shimmering slowly
Over the well-polished aspidistra.

Going to the Pictures

The first time I went to the Waterloo
The subject was Pirates and the hero
—Scion of the English nobility—
Spoke American. With difficulty
I managed the requisite suspension
Of disbelief, following 'The Black Swan'
To its entirely predictable end.
From our Circle seats we had to descend
A dark, smoke-filled staircase where banisters,
Clutched at for guidance, oozed running water.

As we became blasé we disdained it,
Though frequently it was in that fleapit
That the more interesting films were screened.
The Empire and the Coliseum, cleaned
And hygienic, had epics by Metro
And Goldwyn, where we absorbed farragos
Of nonsense as well as Hamlet and some
Great expectations.
              The Coliseum
Can still put on movies but we have lost
Our Empire and our Waterloo and most
Of our pictures are home-viewed.
                  Recently,
In York, for a film specifically
Recommended, with a familiar
Title and a theme very similar
To 'The Red Shoes', we were forced to concur
—Despite the different subject-matter—
That films called 'Black Swan', whatever the ball-
Yhoo, are invariably banal.

Whitby 2011

Featherbed Lane
for Delphine

They cut the roses and the meadowsweet
On the narrowest high-road in England
A yellowhammer gleams and whitethroats bleat

Over wrecked cow parsley and bittersweet
It's dangerous to give a helping hand
They cut the roses and the meadowsweet

All these rough flagstones have been smoothed by feet
A pannierway for horses in their band
A yellowhammer gleams and whitethroats bleat

This path where Granny took us for a treat –
The Stuarts licensed it (for contraband)
They cut the roses and the meadowsweet

I can't remember when we meant to meet
Or if you exercised a countermand
A yellowhammer gleams and whitethroats bleat

Sixty years on, white-haired and with discreet
Walking-sticks, we pick our way down as planned
They cut the roses and the meadowsweet
A yellowhammer gleams and whitethroats bleat.

Warri Board

Unaware of a market hierarchy, we wandered past stalls
Interspersed with sheets laid out on the cobbles, apparently
Set out at random: china, chinoiserie, crockery,
Chandeliers, pot pourri vases, pewter and pieces of eight.

No doubt there were hidden treasures in cardboard boxes
We hadn't got time to leaf through, while the chances of finding
Genuine Delft in the more elegant stalls were just about
Par with turning up even a nineteenth century netsuke.

Once out of the Jeu de Balle, we lingered in Blaestraat,
Intrigued by the sign on the carousel in a shop
Saying Welcome to Mablethorpe, as bizarre as
The painted horses and motorbikes, ready to roll.

What caught my eye in the jetsam of thirty-five
Civilizations, washed up in any old order
But carefully labelled and priced, were the parallel rows
Of six cups, carved from a solid and ancient oblong.

It stood on the floor in a jumble of kitchenware
Crying out for identification and rescue.
The next thing I saw—three figures in euros—I balked at,
But then curiosity made me come back for a closer look.

Half a yard high, it had primitive feet—the whole thing
Chipped from a musty Ghanaian wood, too hard to be
Worm-eaten but longing for beeswax. One side had
Tracery, resembling nothing so much as runes.

Torn, for a moment I wavered. It wasn't so much
The price as the weight which deterred me

But I went on regretting my instincts of common sense
Which told me we had one, unused and unpolished at home.

Our own de-luxe version, elephant-shaped,
Fits (only just) under the gate-legged table. There are
Well over fifty dry beans in its belly and each end
Has another, superfluous, cup for the winnings.

An African game, it began perhaps by the Nile
Where it was easy to scoop out holes in the mud
And make collections of pebbles, presupposing a people
Proficient in counting and having the leisure to play.

Was it carried—maybe by the trading Hausas—
On those treks across the savannah to Western Sudan
At a time when the original slave caravans
Headed North? It was taken across the Atlantic

And was popular in sugar and cotton plantations
Right up to the Second World War when dominoes,
Sadly, dislodged it, though I think it is merchandised
Now in a plastic box. I abandoned my bygone

With a memory of my father, the Senior District Commissioner,
Bored with his office, going down to the market in Kibi
And accepting the challenge of senior market ladies,
Bored with selling bananas, who played him for peanuts.

It took him an age to work out the number of beans
He would move and it was like watching chess between
Grandmaster and novice—the responses came lightning-like
With gales of laughter as, inevitably, he lost.

Variation on a theme by Auden

We ask ourselves Is this the way to go?
Right from the start I wasn't sure I knew.
If I could tell you I would let you know.

Don't make a fuss, don't let your feelings show
(From Nanny's list of things we mustn't do)
We ask ourselves Is this the way to go?

Here is the chart, you can't go wrong, although
That's not a footpath – streams are marked in blue.
If I could tell you I would let you know.

Why don't you save? Why do you act as though
The mortgage payment wasn't overdue?
We ask ourselves Is this the way to go?

How will the dice fall from a careless throw
Can fortune's wheel revolve to something new?
If I could tell you I would let you know.

We made our choices many years ago
Now it's too late – somehow we missed our cue
We ask ourselves Is this the way to go?
If I could tell you I would let you know.

Imperfections 2013
(2013)

Two Goathland Poems

I. Teacher

Miss Patterson can't have cared very much about
Handwriting because mine used to get me into
Trouble almost throughout my secondary school
Education. On the other hand she got me
Reading omnivorously and precociously,
She stirred my interest in natural science
(With tankfuls of jelly which miraculously turned
Into two or three frogs) and somehow she taught me
To think for myself. The only reason I'm sure
About the latter is by eliminating
Everybody else who might have taught me something :
None of them did that so it has to be Miss P.
She taught me for less than a year but I remain
Grateful : I don't remember a lot about her
Except she bicycled to lessons (which I took
With Ann and Shirley who were both older than me)
From an isolated lodge on the moors which she
Shared with her aged father. As a governess
She had little in common with Mary Poppins
Apart from that knowledge of how to make you think—
A kind of magic I would like to have absorbed
When dealing with awkward classes. At least I learnt
Not to care very much about their handwriting.

II.   John likes water

No, not sea beaches, nor even the East Row ram
In Mulgrave Woods—the earliest water hallow
I associate with my childhood was a 'dam'
Which was really a foss on the Murk Esk below

Darnholm—and I discovered it by accident
When pursuing, in the shallows, my reed boat fleet
Downstream. Hardly a cataract but some torrent
For a small boy to think about, getting cold feet

In the process. Once down, the pool had water voles,
Wagtails and a Hairstreak for identifying
In Miss Patterson's book. I must have spent the whole
Of that afternoon alone, intent on grubbing

And fossicking, happily deaf to all voices
Save that of the fall, which I continued to haunt
That summer and, given the chance, still rejoice
To revisit. On the way to Miss Patterson's gaunt

Sometime-home last week, the moorland tarn that we edged
Is my other old shrine, where I first recorded
Dragonflies helicoptering over the sedge
Or chomping innocent mosquitoes in reedbeds,

While wailing peewit screamed round summer picnickers,
Furry caterpillars lumbered through bilberries
And, elsewhere, Sicily and Mussolini were
Hot topics of adult conversazione.

Awkward Age (1946)

In Mulgrave Woods massed ramsons usually
           Swamped rathe primrose
In May. The stink was feral, unlikely.
           Eglantine (those
Shoots were sweet) diverted our visit
           To the river,
Where we swam unsupervised, illicit
           And ashiver

But it was warmer than the sea. The sands
           Were now opened
For exploration—blockhouses, gunstands,
           Stood at the end
Of the links, from which we could sally to
           Find lost golf balls,
Upsetting completely such rendez-vous'
           Courting couples.

When Grandfather embanked Upgang Ravine,
           With hobbit-size
Quarter-mile culvert, did he imagine
           The enterprise
Of his frightened grandson, crawling towards
           A faint nova
Through stagnant pools of rat pee and bat turds,
           All for a dare?

Broad cast-iron arches of Ruswarp Bridge
           Were another
Dare erected by Grandfather, at which
           We would gather
And hesitate. The day I was half-way

Dizzyingly
Up it, the Stationmaster shouted 'Hey'—
So startling me

That I ran headlong to the furthest side
To trudge homeward
Through terra incognita. (At low tide
Spital Bridge ford
Was crossable if its potent odour
Could be washed free
Before teatime.) An earlier venture
On the fishquay

(After we'd clambered down access ladders
To the Scots fleet)
Had revealed to us, under it, wharves where,
On cobbled streets,
Seaweed dripped slime and we could only creep
Like hobgoblins
Among black rats from some abandoned ship
—All aliens.

Moorland tarns acted like distant lodestones
Attracting us
In high summer through purple ling, sheep bones
And old grouse butts.
When a whaup rose wailing, doggedly we
Tracked and retracked
And came upon four eggs eventually,
Olive-mottled

And pear-shaped. Stealthily we crept toward
Our hallowed mere,
With a scatter of gulls and two mallard
Which flew over

The hillcrest, quacking. Why do we recall
Such incidents?
Why do they seem, within a life, more real
Than big events?

Alf and Uncle Robert

It would be hard to find two more different men
Than Alf and Uncle Robert, whose paths must have crossed
And who must have known of each other's existence,
Though I doubt that they ever communicated.

Nor am I sure, when Uncle Robert was selling
Things—houses or secondhand furniture—whether
He had ever wished to live by auctioneering
Or merely accustomed himself to that career.

A shy man, whose diffidence masked a deep knowledge
Of all things pertaining to the area round
Whitby; having survived the war, he took a firm pledge
(With himself) that henceforth he would stay on home ground.

He once told another nephew he spent his war
Coke-stoking—when the army failed to realise
A natural sniper's fieldcraft in wood or moor—
Where, if he took you shooting, it opened your eyes

Not only to gull-flight, plover wail and pigeon
Roost but also matters archaeological:
His Stone Age tools, an astounding collection
In Whitby Museum, are his memorial.

If you saw Alf expertly installing a sink
And deftly adjusting minute screws with fingers

The size of polonies, you might not stop to think
That his mind was at sea with ducks and mergansers,

Plotting the likely landfall of flights of pinkfoot
Or calculating the chance of a backing wind
Before the next morning. If you sailed in his boat
In trout-netting season (Uncle Robert had dinned

It into us never to use the word 'salmon')
You were expected to take your share in the work,
Both rowing and hauling. Alf was the fisherman
Who in Robin Hood's Bay sniffed his course through a roke

Like an antique Maori—knowing each patch of sea
And where it stretched to shore in open-ended lakes.
We would laze on sand at tide-turn, then, wearily
Pull round each sea-loch, splashing our way from the strakes

Deliberately—to frighten our prey netwards
—And so it went on all night. Next day we returned
To plumbing and teaching, with only curt, brief words
Of farewell. If I tried to tot up what I learned

From Robert and Alf, it would be quite difficult
To define a kind of slow-growing awareness
Of my share in a habitat. A crypto Celt
Born in Yorkshire, I spent fifty-odd years careless

Of what made them tick and why they were different:
Like their ganseys—Robert's is practically mint
But too tight for me, while Alf's was time-worn, ancient
And fish-scaled. And perhaps he was buried in it.

Herring Fleet

It was Herodotus who established
The practice of writing about others
And their customs. Why should a native wish
To explain himself or describe matters
Perfectly understood by his comperes?
I am, I suppose, only half-native
Despite being born here, indecisive

And not knowing where to belong, which was
Partly because of the War and partly
The Esk's estuary, dividing us
Between the East and West sides of Whitby.
We knew who was our common enemy
As well as we knew that our East-siders,
Though ours, were unmistakeably other.

Where we met was the quay, a nauseous,
Stinking brouhaha of warring, cursing
Fishermen at work while, on their periplous
Of gaping tourists, small boys filched herring
From glutted creels. They fell, opalescing
On oil-soaked concrete—an invitation
To supplement meagre post-war rations.

We knew our keelboats and the fishermen:
Provider and Endeavour, Pilot Me,
The Storrs and Coles, Nobles and Hutchinsons,
Success and Progress, Venus, Galilee,
Drydens, Dukes, Winspears, Theakers and Leadleys—
But only by repute. Our otherness
Was such as to interdict friendliness . . .

But then, in early autumn, overnight
The port was full of keelboats – you could cross
The river on them if you timed it right
In smocks and wellies, looking officious.
Coming from Campbeltown, their otherness
Was so extreme that I made acquaintance
And, astonishingly, gained acceptance

As a supercargo on Morag Bhan
Because James MacMillan took a liking
To me. Till then, my only perception
Of the Scottish fleet was a host of twinkling
New-bathed stars spreading northwards at evening
From the harbour bar. The reality
Was a fug of diesel, fishguts, body

Odours and a fierce determination
Not to be seasick nor be in the way.
The best place was a far forward station
Wedged in the prow where, quickly, the display
Of lights dispersed and only Venus lay
Below the stars, apart from our partner,
On the shoal James had chosen near Dogger.

We took it in turns to cast and rotate
Around each other so the nets were hauled
Alternately. If James had got it right,
A torrent of silver fish cascaded
Into our hold until we were loaded,
Which could take all night – the sea was teeming
With our stem ploughing through banks of herring

In seemingly endless profusion. Though
Dawn had not broken, we could head due West,
Alone on the ocean. We went below

For bacon and eggs whilst keeping abreast
By radio with events in the rest
Of the fleet. In August and September,
Just for three years—how I still remember!

But the pattern was broken by National
Service. I came home to a token fleet:
A poor memento of irrational
Harvesting was all that was left to greet
Returning soldiers and as for the sweet
Morag, she had been sold to establish
Scientifically the dearth of fish . . .

I was born in September by that sea
Where I still live in a town devoted
Entirely to tourists and memories
They can't share. From the port where I boated
Come the recollected smells, air-floated,
Maybe Icelandic kippers, sharply strong,
To reassure me here's where I belong.

Pinned on a wall in Verona
for Gillian L.

You won't remember me, or if you do
Only because we spent that night fishing
Together on the Dogger Bank—when you
Conquered the crew's aversion to shipping
A woman simply because you were you.
My mannerly devotion was something
You could cope with just as well as you knew
How to partner the skipper, when dancing
A reel on a Saturday night. Maybe
You'll never know how every time I think
Of that lost herring fleet, immediately
I wonder what became of you. I blink
Not a tear for my teenage ignorance
But mourn for your memory's persistence.

Joe Soap and History 2013

One of those useless regrets Mr Macmillan
Advised us not to waste time on can be something
Quite simple like never keeping a diary.
If I had one to look at for nineteen sixty

I wonder what I would find, apart from Finals
And the problems of arranging our nuptials
In France. That April, Kennedy would not appear
Anywhere—except in the files of the Mafia—

Though Gary Powers and Mr Kruschev exist
As names I remember. My tutor would insist
On the writing of essays—despite my social side
I was still unemployed and still unqualified—

So I have absolutely no recollection
Of Eichman's kidnap nor the humiliation
Of Eisenhower in Paris which nearly set off
A Third World War. Did the possibility of

'Some damn silly thing in the Balkans' (provoking
The First) even cross the Edwardians' thinking
I wonder? Insouciance is all very well
When you're young but soon becomes irresponsible

When you don't get a good degree. Nevertheless
The fulfilment of the unforgiving minutes
Can leave you no time for diaries. Would I have then
Scribbled, like the antepenultimate Bourbon,

Fatuously putting 'Nothing', on a day when
His kingdom quaked? My grandmother caused me chagrin

By burning all her memories when she moved house
For the last time but my mother's notes still arouse

Disbelief when used to settle an argument:
(At tragic moments, heroes share the sentiment
Of commoners but don't break up their lines to weep)
Churchill's speech in nineteen forty about hardship

Is recorded right next door to cocktail parties
And dances—and minimises the gravity
Of the nation's state. So how good an idea
Is it to get uptight about North Korea?

Mother Thekla (1918–2011)

Somewhere in Japan there must be old gentlemen
Who still have photographs taken that windswept day
In the nineteen-eighties on the North Yorkshire coast.
There would only be you and Katherine, uncertain
Whether to smile with the Land Rover's passengers,
Earnestly snapping away, communicating
Through a single interpreter and probably
Equally ignorant of each other's beliefs.

I had been (willingly) roped in as a chauffeur,
Which was only one of the roles I played for you—
Along with proof-reader, fisherman, critic and,
Undramatically, friend. Some of our meetings
Remain indelible: I like to recall them,
As on the day of Mother Katherine's funeral,
When your valediction was based on the premise
That the greatest, mortal, crime was stupidity.

Or the day when you looked at one of my essays
And simply pulled a face and, at my asking why,
You quoted your barrister father whose mantra
Was 'Do not overstate your case'. All great teachers
Remain at the back of our consciousness for life.
Best of all I remember our daughter, riding
The moor and calling in at the monastery
To show off her new pony. On Maundy Thursday.

Long before she came home you had telephoned me,
Profuse with apologies, maybe forgetting
Mother Maria's dictum on the importance
Of allowing young people the freedom to stray . . .

There had to be limits, like the absolute ban
On discussing your war (with your fluent Russian
You were marked to be mentioned in dispatches
And one would have liked to have known more than
　'the WAAFs').

I still have a guilty conscience for losing touch.
What brought you to me last week was finding, behind
A triptych by Memling, St Mary of Egypt,
Subject of one of your books I don't need to read:
I know how you existed on that bleak hillside,
Meeting only at lunch, saying your offices
Six times a day. Monotony in your life freed
The spirit, enabling you to pray for the world.

March 2013

Easter Things

We needed onion skins and cochineal
With the limited egg-ration:
Enough to make us feel
The occasion
And peel
With care
The bright fragments
Being very aware
Of the annual sacrament
Which brought the whole tribe together to share.

For Simon and Ali and Nick we hid
A few dozen multicoloured
Shells carelessly amid
The rhubarb bed
And did
Not guess
At how they might
Remember—and address
Their own offspring towards the rite,
Bind them to egg-hunt in the Easter process.

Earnshaw and other household gods.
for Roy Clarke

When Compo died I was worried
That they might go over the top
With a 'bad Dickens'– type deathbed—
The Old Curiosity Shop

Springs to mind—but, amazingly,
Equilibrium was maintained:
Delicate lines between schmaltzy
And limpid poignancy remained

Clear. The character humour
Shafts were timed to relieve tension:
Dragons were shorn of their armour,
Pearl became suddenly human

And we became conscious that, were
One to DNA them—Compo
And Clegg —they might have had forebears
Dwelling round here in AD two.

Blamire and Foggy and Seymour
Each seemed foreign or 'incoming'
(Means you don't talk like your neighbour)
And their successors were lacking

Reality. A down to earth
Celebration—dulce domum
For basic tykes—half a crown's worth,
Maybe, of late chrysanthemums

Was offered speculatively—
With bad language, permanent smokes,
And no special anxiety
For audience laughter at jokes.

But (like 'Pickwick') it hit a chord
And it seemed that quite suddenly
We all knew Edie and Howard,
Who moved in a modern Dingley

Dell, where a Winkle might mingle
With Ivy, Nora and Weller
And, certainly, Alfred Jingle
Could walk out of Nohall, Nowhere.

To say that it didn't last is
Ridiculous—no doubt it went
On too long. Apotheosis,
Achieved with the wellies lament,

Would have been a fitting last shout.
Instead, the fading old soldiers
Continued to drill and went out
Not with a bang but a whimper.

Andrew at the airport

I didn't see you at first. My party,
Made up, I suppose, of my immediate
Family, was shouting amicably,
All unaware of the one isolate
Seated figure with a full breakfast plate,
Who made no answer to my pleased 'Now then!'
I woke: you went. I cried to dream again.

We had maybe a dozen years knowing
Each other precisely : the mid-fifties,
With me touring Europe, you returning
To Africa, decreed that henceforth we
Just met at airports occasionally.
Our inescapable roads' divergence
Could not split a friendship of commonsense,

With no need to say 'Do you remember?'
Unless we wanted to check on somebody
Else's mythology. To foregather
At Durham Tees Airport was ritually
A dawn observance—therefore normally
We ought to have been together eating:
The sorrow of dreams lies in awaking.

There was the time you landed in shorts
And an open-necked shirt with the question
How well you might pass in wealthy resorts
As an international banker? And then
Dropped in to chat to your friend the Chairman
(Raised eyebrows in Gracechurch Street). But you were
True to yourself—and if our grandfather

Had been around I could see him nodding
Approval. You earned my own at Kai Tak
—At least ten years later—by just being
There, a solid figure amidst chiyack
And uncaring chaos, who seized my pack,
Guiding me through the post-imperial
Endless customs of banking protocol.

The enduring thing was our amity.
Before you joined me at school I'd been there
Three years and they asked if you were like me
And I said 'No, not at all', unaware
Of how unmistakeably our forebears
Had marked us. They laughed but our resemblance
Altered with age and mutual tolerance.

What you liked was visiting castles, when
I was the host who could sometimes supply
Historical details with acumen
If not always tout à fait exactly.
I would culture-switch absent-mindedly
Or sit in a hide recording bellbirds
While you were solving Telegraph crosswords.

Wellington airport's as bleak and windswept
As Spurn Head (that last time when, together,
We had spent a day touring but had kept
No photos like those from Cape Palliser
Taken nearly twenty years earlier):
If I knew at a glance how the meeting
Would end, we managed a normal greeting—

What you might call the usual Ave
In Yorkshire. We had no last messages
Like how much we would miss our palavers
By telephone—and only two aunties
Left to send love to—a shy quietus.
'You're leaving for another Timbuktu?
So long then'. Maybe this gives life to you.

Relativity

There's some doubt about the veracity
    Of incidents
Found in *The Story of San Michele*.
    When Axel went
To Lapland, for example, and he met
    The curious
Little gnome, what does our modern mindset
    Reject, refuse?

It's a parable not that difficult
    To understand.
The goblin's reaction to the occult
    Gold watch's hands
Mocks time which, as we all know, is contained
    In the present
Where future and past are also maintained.
    The incessant

Tick is nothing of which to be afraid—
    The Cretan glance,
Or the Spartan, sitting to wash his braids,
    Each gives a chance

To get ready—and readiness is all
    Whether it be
Now or some day tomorrow—it's a call
    That certainly

There is no ignoring. Axel's goblin,
    I think, would not
Have come across the Essays of Montaigne,
    Nor even thought
Of time, save as another dimension
    Wherein to make
Merry, enjoy the human condition,
    Sleep, and awake.

Two Minutes Hate—April 2013

I. Ukelele Song

Now André Rieu is a fiddle man
Playing sweet and sugary notes.
He'll fiddle all day in a sickly way
To really get one's goat.
He plays his tunes with a smarmy grin
For he's reckoned he cannot lose:
All day he'll smirk and play the birk
And that's why I'm singing the blues—

Chorus:
Oh André Rieu, what shall I do?
I really hate your oleaginous stew.
Its sickly feeling leads me to appealing
Oh won't you flush your fiddle down the loo?

There used to be a Sky Arts Programme Two
With operas and plays and concerts too.
Now Strauss is everlasting as his waltz continues blasting:
There's no escaping endless Sky Arts Rieu.

Chorus:
Oh André Rieu . . .

A Liberace with a violin
Picked out his target à la Vera Lynn.
The Danube's so polluted that the blue has been transmuted:
It's like a mushy sludge of harlequin.

Chorus:
Oh André Rieu . . .

II. Huis Clos—an Epitaph

We shopkeepers must be judged just
As guilty as she. Somebody,
Somewhere, ought to have had the guts
Not to vow to thee, my country

But we all got carried away,
Got stuck in the decennial
Of a new July Monarchy
Which put greed on a pedestal

And flushed charity down the drain.
Reaction now is faraway
Too late, but one can imagine
A room where she's obliged to play

Her part for all eternity
With two men—certainly Scargill
For one. Add Brucie, to really
Make the trio unbearable.

Sestina from the Pontic Steppe

William of Rubruk had to hire his waggons,
Making his way through boundless earth and stars,
With glimpses of the Don beyond the grass
And bluegreen plants like wormwood, rue and thyme.
No threat then were the marauding Cossacks
(Short commons were the norm but he was young

And healthy : the Franciscans were a young
Order to which he had hitched his waggon)
Despite grave warnings of the Tartar sacks,
Haruspications, junctions of the stars –
He slept all night on bergamot and thyme,
Inching his way across unending grass.

Russian incursions brought the death of grass.
The Soviet demise has left the young
Caught in a vortex of suspended time,
Where tractors have replaced antique waggons
So clouds of petrol fumes blot out the stars
And roads are strewn with empty plastic sacks.

The Mongol Khanate had renounced its sacks
Establishing a culture built on grass
Where William navigated by the stars.
Nature reserves are relatively young
Phenomena. How can ox and waggon
Plod the last syllable of space-age time

Through poppy-fields and straggling meads of thyme
When Man's fierce maw insists on more wheat-sacks?
Sparse rye-fields William saw from his waggon
And Cuman tumuli amidst the grass

'Two leagues off' broke a horizon, the young
Friar noted, only defined by stars.

Conversion of the heathen was the star
He hitched his ox to for the umpteenth time
Unavailingly, compliant like young
Chekhov, astronomising on the sacks
Six hundred years later, cruising the grass,
Dreaming of cherry orchards in his ox-waggon.

When Chekhov was young, his ox-drawn waggon
Sailed through waves of thyme in oceans of grass:
He lay on wheat-sacks, gazing at the stars.

A Propos from Alain

It seems that Queen Victoria used to enjoy
A trip to the beach, where she had a contraption
In which she could bathe secluded from prying eyes
And sheltered from the more exuberant breakers.

Whether or not this was public knowledge remains
Obscure but whoever set the trend, it seems clear
That the seaside habit begun in the last years
Of her reign is part of our holiday ethic.

Contraptions are not a regal monopoly
But it does seem extraordinary nowadays
How bulky impedimenta seem essential
In the urge to build fortifications in sand—

A shifting, volatile element, half-liquid,
Where signs are quickly rubbed out, beyond which stretches
That heaving mass in which no signs are possible.
A place where something ends and something else begins.

When you sit on a beach, watching wave succeeding
Wave, it's the negation of human influence:
Chaos begins and it might be an idea
To eschew sun-bathing for consideration

Of one's own unimportance. You have two choices:
You can go back to sleep or start building empires,
Cloud-capped towers, gorgeous palaces, in the waves.
In the woods there is fear, something mysterious,

But there are sacred signs and symbols to read there
Which we need to interpret. At sea, the least furl
On the end of a breaker has significance
Equal to the crash of an Atlantic roller:

Nothing is big or little because what is big
Is only drops of water moulded together
Purposelessly and wildly boxing the compass.
By the seaside, Nature's no longer frightening

Because she has no recognisable features.
Man, emerging from his forest, comes to terms with
The redoubtable, comprehensible ocean,
Which is, I suppose, when he starts to dare to think.

Ballade of the last Englishman

On rereading *A Month in the Country*
For the fourth or fifth time, I'm still puzzled
By the narrative's fearful symmetry.
I can't find 'He shal com with woundes rede
To deme the quikke and the dede' recorded
Anywhere—ballad or mystery play?
How educated guesses can't betray
The real Alice, the lives of the Great War's
Survivors, even about Judgement Day:
I'd like to talk to Mr J. L. Carr.

Familiar heroes from history
Crop up, appearing when least expected:
Harpole and Foxberrow, the life story
In eight sections, is at last concluded
With chapter headings wholly selected
From 'Horatius' as told by Macaulay,
But *A Day in Summer* brings into play
Benaiah, the son of Jehoiada,
Who slew a lion on a snowy day:
I'd like to talk to Mr J. L. Carr.

The pupils chanting 'Loveliest of trees'
At Easter I ought to have adopted.
I could have eschewed the purgatory
Of staff meetings if only I had read
That he never held them. How he treated
A book called *Henry Moore* was an essay
In avoiding the subject, to portray
The man who had been their joint Headmaster
(Who'd marched a band down the Champs Elysées):
I'd like to talk to Mr J. L. Carr.

Improper lines from Flecker, virelays
Against the desecration of old, grey
Churches, showing things as they really are,
Would give material to pass the day:
I'd like to talk to Mr J. L. Carr.

R.I.P.

It seems strange that in two thousand and one
A Lady should bother about seating
At table. (Given a conversation
Lively enough or a happy meeting
Of minds, in vulgar terms, who gives a toss?)
You would think precedence had been defunct
Since about the middle of the Great War
                        With the asinine loss
Of five million young men, grotesquely junked
On the scrapheap of Europe's battlefloor.

But, like the last Bourbons, Lady Powell
Has learnt nothing and forgotten nothing:
Though her fierce vignette of Lady Christabel
May be nearer to Proust than anything
Accomplished by her husband, Anthony,
Over twelve volumes. In Search of Lost Time
Is timeless in the pitiless satire
                        Which unforgettably
Depicts a social world beyond its prime
In a Paris under German shellfire.

The extraordinary thing was how
It was quite possible for him to dine
At restaurants like the Ritz or Ciros
On beef à la mode or soles in white wine,

With Zeppelins and Gothas overhead
And a bombardment which was audible
Across the Channel. You might say there were
                Laws for the privileged
Which were just as unintelligible
To the humble as reasons for the War.

Those O.R.s in the fraternisation
Of Christmas fourteen only narrowly
Escaped court martial. They ought to have been
Exterminating a German army
Of men much like themselves. The no man's land
Between Ours and Theirs was immutable,
As was the inexplicable useage
                Giving the high command
Powers which made all things permissible
To classes with money and lineage.

In that Great War sweet old Aunt Lucy knew
Just what everybody was fighting for,
My own sweet Aunt Lucy hadn't a clue
Why she was fighting the Second World War
As a WAAF. Though the power balance
By then had shifted ineluctably,
Our kingdom must have been more united
                After the fall of France
And the Blitz than any time possibly
Since the imperial dream was floated.

The Empires' hapless disintegration
Meant the end of a feudal society
Where precedence counted. No man,
As Chaucer observed, 'as man may well see',
Can bequeath true gentilesse to his heirs:
An idea from the *Convivio*,

Though undoubtedly it had been current
                    From Christian Caesars
Onwards. Our trouble is that we have no
Acceptable civilised replacement.

If we have to laugh unbelievingly
At the late Lady's sublime ignorance
Of the classless twenty-first century
Place we inhabit, the indifference
Of most of the population to what
Offended her is, historically,
Important. In two thousand and fourteen
                    No Sarajevo shot
Could make men die patriotically
At the mere behest of a king or queen.

A Metalogue to Puccini's La Rondine

Puccini's *La Rondine* was first staged
In nineteen seventeen. Disadvantaged
Right from the start by preoccupation
With the Western Front, the presentation
In neutral Monte Carlo did nothing
To stir interest. What was more galling
For the claque was a lack of tragedy
And their perception, unforgivably,
Of a libretto void of silliness:
It flopped because of its ordinariness.

And yet it is extraordinary,
Perhaps because of the reality
Of its demi-monde milieu frequented
By poets testing the rich and titled
As patrons of the arts. We recognise
In Magda Swann's Odette but sympathise
With her rather than him. It's a world where
Wealth is already the guiding factor
Through sad remains of aristocracy
In an opulent fin de siècle soirée.

We all know 'Nessun dorma' nowadays
(Because of that World Cup); and 'One Fine Day'
Is almost as familiar a tune
As it was in my youth. But the unknown
Quartet from Act Two of *La Rondine*
(Which lasts three minutes) has a melody
More beautiful than either. What happens
When Magda reads the letter enlightens
Our understanding of love, her gesture
Leaves us, somehow, cathartically pure.

25th August 2013

Trisha brought you a bunch of red roses
Which you thrust carelessly into a pot
On the sideboard. To look such gift-horses
In the mouth, your instinctive trait, may not
Be exactly convenable but it's part
Of your charm, as is your tendency to
Stray from an argument's point but my heart,
Enfin, is yours. If we upset those who
Are not used to dialectics, tant pis—
And tant pis, too, for all the wails and shouts.
I think of the girl I brought home fifty-
Five years ago whom, though Mother had doubts,
My father took straight to the verandah
To give his dim roses some ideas.

Chain Reaction
(2015)

1. Hospital Odyssey

A Sonnet Sequence

1. (Shipwreck : Books V and XII)

Much have I travelled: if you think Homer
Exaggerates his hero's endurance
You discover ten days without sleep on
The ward is part of the healing process.
No doubt Ulysses grew familiar
With knots in his mast as I to odd, chance
Views of Fred's privates with diapason
Of Geordie's revolting excrescences.
Where you go at night depends on nurses:
Nausikaa's, Circe's, Calypso's islands,
Olympus or Troy with blood and curses:
You learn to know the good ones, endure commands
Of unreasoning Gods of fate and doom
And lie, unsleeping, in the dimlit room.

II. (The Suitors : Book I)

Like Telemachus we are troubled by
Uninvited suitors. Rules and advice
Mean nothing to the Starkadders who swarm,
Unthinking, through visiting hours around
Their patriarch next door. The reasons why
Might well be the suitors': greed, avarice,
A hint of affection. Raising a storm
Was always some god's job but here the sound
Of alarm bells gets little attention.
The cleanliness obsession was clearly
Part of upper-class Bronze Age convention
Still here, thank God, treated seriously.
Looting and piracy, incest and rape,
Are customs we have managed to escape.

III. (The Lotus Eaters : Book IX)

When those sailors were tempted to walk out
In Lotus land, Ulysses drove them back to
The ship, thereby saving their lives. It's short,
That passage, and you can't help wondering
If it wasn't self-interest—his drought
Of oarsmen was grave—getting them anew
His only option. I had this thought
At three a.m. as I lay there wishing
I could toss and turn but incapable
Of either, wishing an alternative,
Like Lotus land, were still attainable,
If only one could try it out and live—
Not sure that even if it were, I'd dare
To stake my life on something strange and rare?

IV. *(Women : Books IV and XXIII)*

Apart from the goddesses, the women
Are minor figures: Helen beautiful,
Penelope faithful, but otherwise
We know little about them, nor do they
Act as nurses after the battles. When
Olivia came to help she was full
Of confidence, transmitted through her eyes
Which were unsentimental, staid, that day
She changed my various dressings but gave
Me no pain. As she adjusted the bands
I wanted to thank her so said 'You have
Delicate hands. You have delicate hands.'
Repeating it to make my meaning clear
While smiling to relax the atmosphere.

V. *(Ghosts : Book XI)*

I went with Ulysses to meet the ghosts,
Awoke Achilles from his last long sulk,
Thought of how he and Hector both took flight
When it was prudent, did not hesitate
To use the bow if possible, when hosts
Of armies clashed amidst the burnt-out hulks.
Swarming from Erebus' perpetual night
The shades continued to bemoan their fate.
Then it was Jo-Maria shaking me
Gently awake and posing the question:
'Where have you been?', asking repeatedly,
With some amusement: 'Where have you been, John?'
How could I tell them that my mind had been
Where we might all end? How could I begin?

VI. (Lies : Books IX, XIII and XIV)

When Shakespeare's Ulysses pontificates
About right and wrong, it's strange how he seems
To forget the wily Grecian hero
Who sacks Ismarus, killing all the men
And sharing the loot, does not hesitate
To lie to Athene-whose-eye-gleams
And his own swineherd: indeed his motto
Invariably seems to have been 'When
In doubt, tell lies.' I'm sure nobody here
Would tell me something untrue but sometimes
Feel too reassured. 'It will get better'.
'You will get used to it.' Passing my time
Between catheter, drain and stomach-bag,
It might be easier to live in drag.

VII. (Straits of Messina : Book XII)

It is difficult to identify
Places which existed well over three
Thousand years ago but most scholars choose
The Straits of Messina for Scylla's lair
And the whirlpool of Charybdis, but why
Ulysses had to thread them twice, as we
Know, has to do with sea-levels and those
Earthquakes through history so common there.
He went East to West with most of his crew
But returned alone on his mast, to land
On Calypso's isle, where he was compelled to
Stay seven years (—it's thought, a small island
Off Sicily). Twelve days in hospital,
I reckon, sometimes can seem eternal.

VIII. (Ithaca : Book XIII)

And where is Ithaca? Apparently
Not where it's placed in the atlas. It seems
That Cephalonia's peninsula
On its eastern coast was in Homer's day
An island, matching all the geography
Detailed by him most knowledgeably. Gleams
Of perception pierce the common aura
Of ignorance, misnomers: pinpoint bay
And headland, olive-grove, pigfarm, palace,
In Paliki, which was Ulysses' home,
A mixture of thin scrub and dense taigas
With rocky outcrops. Where he started from.
Where I started from, where I saw the light—
They'll send me back there in the next fortnight.

IX. (Haven : Book V)

When you're destitute, far from home,
Fearful for your safety, it's a good thing
To find a sure refuge, which Ulysses
Did on Phaeacia, naked and alone.
Thus he met Nausikaa, who chanced to roam
Beside his grove, and did his flattering
Best. Under her aegis he's put at ease
In her house, soon telling all he has done.
I gaze across at Fred, watching TV,
And Geordie visited by wife and child
—He's turned his telly up illegally—
(Compared with Starkadders that's only mild).
What are these gulfs across our common tongue
Which make outlandish communication?

X. (Ablutions : Book VI)

Behind his leafy bough, our sailor
Presented himself to the young princess
But then immediately begged consent
To wash himself in private. Convention
Should then have had one of the handmaids or
Slavegirls anoint him with oil, which was less
Of a cleanser than an emollient,
But, with Athene's help, the ablution
Was completed and Ulysses transformed.
For two days I was helpless and Mary
Drew curtains around before she performed
Lavage on available bits of me.
I must abandon all sense of pudeur,
Do what she says and be grateful to her.

XI. (Dante : Book XI)

To put our much-enduring man in Hell
With the fraudulent—Dante's decision—
To me seems anachronistic, in fact
Very unfair. Ulysses, remember,
Came home alone, so how can Dante tell
Us he set forth with a band of seamen
'Who had never left him' just to enact
A voyage, perhaps beyond the Equator,
In quest of knowledge and virtue? Canto
Twenty-six is renowned as a passage
But it's strange that Dante seems to have no
Knowledge of old Tiresias' presage.
Thoughts of a tired, sick, ex-academic
At three a.m. and with no means to check.

XII. *(the sere, the yellow leaf : Book XXIII)*

Ulysses in slippers and cardigan
(Matched by an aged wife) by the fireside
Is not a view of the heroic age
Most people accept, even though we're pleased
To achieve it. His role as Everyman
As mooted by Joyce is inclined to slide
Into flocci-nocchi type verbiage,
Parodies by which we're perplexed and teased.
What is heroic about Bloom that day
In Dublin is his patience and his quest
For information, his confident way
Of caring for Stephen, self-interest
Aside. Slippers and cardigan now are
Garments with which I've become familiar.

XIII. *(Nestor : Book III)*

Despite his reputation for wisdom
Nestor, it seems to me, bears a startling
Likeness to Polonius: nonetheless
He managed to get home safely
Quicker than anyone else. Advice from
Another time-worn man was just the thing
Telemachus needed if Ulysses
Still lived. Nestor lacked curiosity
—That trait Eliot probably borrowed
From Dante ('not cease from exploration')
And has, for some reason, since been bestowed
On Ulysses' own repatriation
Quest. Myself, I'm apprehensive about
Going home in a state of sheer self-doubt.

XIV. (Zeus : Books V and XII)

Calypso was not pleased with the message
Hermes brought her from all-powerful Zeus
Whose acts quite often seem illogical
When he needs to be reminded of things.
Our own omnipotent's daily passage
Is unpredictable and he's cautious
About promises but amicable,
His judgements, when made, unhesitating.
When Zeus said Ulysses was going home,
He went and, eventually, arrived.
When Doug said 'Home on Sunday' that meant from
Three p.m. we waited for discharge, strived
To contain ourselves. Eventually
We too left, letterless, but homed safely.

XV. (Lists : Books XI and XV)

Ancestral worship's the commentary
Normally given for the lists of names
(Remember 'Harry the King, Bedford
And Exeter etcetera') but they're
Easily skipped. Unlike the Odyssey,
My story's full of heroines: no games
Of derring-do but (hasten to record)
Infinite patience from Maria, Clare
(One and two), Jo, Angela and Tracey,
Olivia and Sarah plus the skill of Doug
Plus Phil's and Andy's practicality.
They fear the menace of the superbug
And fight their battles on the body's sores;
Heroines, heroes of internal wars.

XVI. (Beds : Book XXIII)

Penelope's doubts were only resolved
When Ulysses showed anger for his bed
Of living olive—and that convinced her—
All was harmony. I've been home a week
And though my doubts have been dissolved
About equipment, it's the peace instead
Of tumult I can't take altogether:
As far as sleep's concerned, the outlook's bleak:
So I reread the Odyssey. It's strange
To ponder this three thousand year old tale
Of Ulysses' homecoming to his grange
And think, bemused, of the historical
Background in England. Our ancestors then
Were making votive offerings at Flag Fen.

2. Fenland Aubade

Autumnal mists from reeking fens choked courts and yards
Through much of my first term. Missing our northern haars,
One dawn I went bird-watching to Wicken. Howard,
A Freshman ornithologist, who lived downstairs

And knew the ropes, guided me most sapiently,
Naming Shoveler and Pintail as we threaded
Between buckthorn, sedge and reeds, quietly
Inching into an alien domain, unchanged

For up to three millennia, before which there
Were, apparently, forests. Heading for Burwell,
We saw Greenfinch and Brambling, a Yellowhammer,
Godwits and snipe plus chrysalids of Swallowtails,

Enough for one morning. Fifty years on, chance brought
Me back there as the guiding ornithologist
Of a group and we saw very much the same sort
Of species with Fieldfare and Reed Bunting. The list

Was not identical but similar enough
To be remarked on. It's a mysterious region
Which doesn't show up on a map, stretching in rough
From Cambridge to Peterborough and Huntingdon.

If you look very closely, the legend 'The Fens'
Is found between March and Chatteris. The main town
Is Ely, a fairly modern development
Compared with the Flag Fen walkway, which has been shown

To have been receiving votives in mid-Bronze Age
England. I won't go back. Si jeunesse savait, si
Vieillesse pouvait – as hath it some French sage,
Still reminiscing in old age remorselessly.

3. Sleeping out

I think it must have been a very hot night when,
Sleeping out at Magdalene in the late Twenties, Empson
Could have been in his own bed. But why then did he
Proceed to write it up so impenetrably?

Both acts were volitional, whereas my own
Nights under stars invariably occurred when
I had only a sleeping-bag and no money.
The first time, aged seventeen, on Fiesole

Because it was stifling in the tent I, sneaking
Under an olive, only woke at the creaking
Of a pair of white oxen, ploughing a furrow
In our field, an unforgettable memento.

A five-year gap found me one summer, on my own,
Exploring various haystacks in the Dordogne,
While studying its Romanesque churches, trying
To survive on a pound a day—and managing.

Haystacks are free but leave you looking untidy
And even generous drivers are unlikely
To pick up tramps. Yet still you weigh up the mildewed
Ceiling, lumpy mattress, cost and the multitude

Of bedbugs against a crown of stars, the soft hay,
Peace with infrequent nightingales, even the bray,
On one occasion, of a donkey which awoke
Me opportunely as a farmer tried his choke.

And four years later I returned but with a tent
And a wife who was clever at hitching. We went
From Rossignol to Civrac in our first full day
And slept on the floor of an empty farm. Our way

Haphazard, traversed Gironde. Twice I crept outside
Because of the heat: in a vineyard camp beside
A spring which lulled me to sleep; again by the mere
Of a lost domain whose name I can't remember

Though I can't forget the place or the galaxies
Above. Without a tent, some two years later, we
Walked around Corsica, using steep mountainsides
And endless white sand beaches, out of reach of tides,

To sleep. Near Sartène we awoke to find we were
On the edge of a cliff. On another night, where
Sands shelved sharply, we were dazzled by blinding light
From a rowboat approaching our beach. In sheer fright

I shouted 'Que faites-vous?' and was urgently bade
Not to frighten the fish and the (illegal) raid
Continued happily as we went back to sleep.
Another beach, at dawn, had scouts doing a keep

Fit class, so we had to stay in our sleeping-bags
Until their leader was satisfied. They marched, flags
Flying, back to their camp and we made our final
Hitchhike to Ajaccio's ship ferry terminal.

4. Night Ferry

Was it Huysmans, whose hero, en route to London,
Decided, after a long fog-bound evening in
A café at Gare Saint-Lazare, to abandon
His project and go home? He reasoned he had eaten

Oxtail soup, smoked haddock, roast beef and potatoes,
Surrounded by Englishmen discussing weather,
And had therefore experienced most of those
Essentially English matters then and there.

In the eighteen-eighties he would not have detrained
At Victoria till the next day's afternoon
Whereas we, in the swinging sixties, entertained
Ourselves to dinner in Paris, enjoyed moon-

Lit rides to the Gare du Nord and slept, till daylight
Found us rolling through Kent with an English breakfast
In prospect. Those were the days – or rather the nights –
We look back to nostalgically, even if last

Time we did Paris-Whitby by Chunnel took less
Than ten hours. In the eighties/nineties we became
Used to the Aberdeen–Lerwick voyage, with darkness
A couple of hours around midnight—and the same

Was true of Hull-Bergen. We would sea-watch for hours
Counting gannet and skua, phalarope and tern,
Porpoise, dolphin and Minke whale—all these were ours
To marvel at, chat of to others in the stern.

If you take the ferry from Hull to Zeebrugge
And then go to Bruges or Ghent you must not dare wish
Your French, however fluent, to be de rigueur—
Museum and Gallery signs are in Flemish

Which can be irritating in the otherwise
Perfect new Museum of Archaeology.
In Brussels, no such problems, and we patronise
Hotels which, at the weekend, incline to empty

And are glad to accommodate you. Moreover,
The standards of cuisine are appreciably
Higher and we almost roll back to Zeebrugge
And the mystic charm of another night ferry.

5. Charon

The idea of another world to which a guide
Could be paid to convey you (what, nowadays,
We might call a parallel universe), is as old
As those hills in Wales from which one tribe
Of our ancestors somehow transported Preseli
Bluestone blocks some hundred and fifty miles to build
A part of Stonehenge. Those maps of liminal zones
Of the quick and the dead (the ancestors) add little
To our understanding but seem to share the idea
Of a river—call it Avon or Styx—as a definitive
Boundary.
          Why do I think of Bunyan and how,
When he had passed the waters, 'these trumpeters
Saluted Christian and his fellow with ten thousand
Welcomes from the world'?
                      And, even more strangely,
How did it come to Ulysses to pass into the underworld
Without the assistance of Charon, who's not even mentioned?
The only two tourists who seem to have crossed without
Paying the miserly boatman were Orpheus, whose music
Had charms, and Hercules, whose arms were all too
Evident.
         The location of Hades' gate has given rise
To much argument though 'somewhere in Sicily'
Seems to be favoured by scholars. When you come
To the bourns of those undiscovered countries
They are shifting, fluid and open to contradiction
—Unlike Wordsworth's little Maid who insisted
Steadfastly, politely and firmly 'We are seven'.
At Stonehenge, one imagines some kind of shaman
Conducting a ritual transfer at appointed times
Of the year. The symbolism of our distant forebears

Ceremonially making offerings of valuable swords
And wheels to the Avon or Fenland waters can, possibly,
Be linked to the one obol fee for the ferry of Styx
When you realise that these activities seem to have been
Going on roughly contemporaneously
At the opposite ends of Europe.
                              It continues
To surprise me that Charon should prove to be
Such a comparatively minor figure.

6. *Jasmine and Ursula*

Mitochondrial DNA,
It seems, has conclusively proved
That a mother called Ursula
From Greece, who was born, lived and loved,

One hundred and fifty thousand
Years back, can now count eleven
Percent of Europeans (and
Others) from her generation.

Some of them came to West Britain
By way of the Frisians (I'm not
Sure how) where they formed liaisons
With the issue of Jasmine's lot—

Seventeen percent—who, it's thought,
Came through Iberia. Again,
One asks oneself, how? There's no doubt
A teacher, a Somerset man,

Of the twenty-first century
In Cheddar was found descended
From a Cro-Magnon who, maybe,
Lived there but originated

From Ursula. The conclusions
One draws is that they are mythic,
Those waves of advance, invasions
Of our lands by neolithic

Migrations and, quite possibly,
The Celts never existed as
One cultural identity.
We're left with a multi-tribed place

With a babel of strong accents:
A man from Kent could not follow
A Northumbrian's argument;
-—It's not so very different now.

7. Whose side are you on?

I only knew one set of my Welsh grandparents
Because my father's pair both died before my birth.
My grandfathers—brothers—who hailed from Llandinam
Both must have had Welsh accents, my maternal one's
Only slight: he lived out twenty-five Yorkshire years
With the grandmother I knew very well—so well
That 'Pass me the towel'(two syllables, accent
On the second) is the way I like to recall
Her and my racial origins. Both my parents
Were born in Wales but that doesn't make me a Celt.
Indeed, one has to ask, how do you define one?
I have read somewhere that the Celts are a fairly
Recent invention, not more than a hundred and fifty
Years old. Who the Celts were, according to one authority,
Does not matter much but in that case, how did Yeats
Emerge from their twilight and how did that differ
From the swirling Art Nouveau type pots with divisions
And sub-divisions within a staggering series
Of artefacts from all over Europe? Others talk
Vaguely about 'fortified hilltop 'towns'
Like Celtic oppida settlements in the north
And west of Europe'. Still others assume a race

With an omniscient élite and pre-Roman
System of long straight roads and speedy means
Of communication—oral ones—amazing
Theories with a minimum of archaeological proof.
What undoubtedly existed before the truly miraculous
Growth of Roman engineering was a highly-developed,
Recognisable Iron Age art form as well as
A heterogeneous collection of fables which,
Like Homer's, took a considerable time to be written down
And which, unlike Homer, are almost unreadable
To-day (except to the academic, writing his thesis).
Forebears are always elusively out of reach
And these more than most. But I'd like to DNA
Any distant relations who might, for all I know,
Be still living somewhere around Llandinam.

8. Patriot Games
I.

To-day's junkmail brought a flier
With five grinning faces. They used
To be councillors but they were
Voted out. Bold as brass, they're fused

Now under UKIP—ignorant
Of Sam. Johnson's aphorism
Associating the arrant
Scoundrel with patriotism

As his last refuge. Do they think
The electorate will buy it?
If it's the European link
That scares them, it's a little bit

Weird to think that our Angles rowed
Over from Schleswig, with Saxons
Just to their West. Why did shiploads
Of Jutes quit Denmark to land on

Our shores? Historians seem sure
About their pottery but don't
Seem to know where the pressure
Was coming from and therefore won't

Commit themselves. No one questions
The Normans but does UKIP
Realise we're Europeans
By DNA, race and worship?

Bunch of scoundrels they well may be
In our present Houses but does
Anyone realise fully
How UKIP could prove disastrous?

8. Patriot Games
II.

Either I misinterpreted the history
Text book or simply got it wrong but I always
Believed that Wordsworth wrote 'Bliss was it in that dawn'
As a spontaneous reaction to the Bastille
Assault, whereas it was eighteen o nine before
He got round to recollecting, presumably
In tranquillity. Coleridge too had problems,
As evidenced by his Nether Stowey poem
Of seventeen ninety-eight, when French invasion
Threatened, in which, having managed to think of them
As the enemy, he couldn't control his views
Of the Commons 'Speech-mouthing, speech-reporting Guild
One Benefit-Club for mutual flattery'
But then felt obliged to confess that 'There lives nor
Form nor feeling in my soul unborrowed from my
Country', evoking the church tower and four huge elms
Of 'beloved Stowey' in a conversation
Piece which, surprisingly, becomes patriotic.

9. On not reading Shakespeare's Sonnets in hospital

I.

How careful was I when I took my way
To choose three books I thought I could reread,
To pleasurably pass long hours of day
Revisiting the urgent calls to breed,
The sugar'd lines among his private friends,
Familiar phrases, unlooked for tropes,
New insights into what the verse intends,
The stark nullification of his hopes.
A convalescence would be more the time
(I see Jack Lewis reading Jean de Meun)
To retread then the primrose paths of rhyme.
What e'er the case, the sonnets lay alone,
Unread. As if I didn't know the score
But, knowing what I knew, abjuring more.

II.

Why is my verse so barren of new pride,
Clothing itself in tried and tested forms?
The string the pearls were strung on, the inside
Carpet figure, undoubtedly performs
More than the sum of its parts, like two streams'
Confluence. Rhyme, stanza-shape and metre,
Are only exo-skeletons for dreams
Or rich phantasies of lotus-eaters.
Love is a luxury you can't afford
When age and sickness grab you by the throat,
Stifle all feeling save one's need to hoard
The little you have left and learn by rote
The mantras of survival. Drink and eat,
Sleep, if you can, and exercise your feet.

III.

What's in the brain that ink may character?
To recollect in home's tranquillity
How very ill I was—so that only Homer's
Odyssey had kinds of reality
I could read and enjoy. I don't recall
Any vows but began to write within a day
Of homecoming. It was by no means all
Plain sailing but I knew where my route lay.
The composition was therapeutic
Between bouts of the crossword, taking
Prescribed pills and snacks, quite fatalistic
About the results and the creating
Of something which began to have its own
Momentum, almost, progressing alone.

IV.

As a decrepit father takes delight
In all his progeny may undertake,
Lauds their ability to find the right
Answer to storms in his teacups, earthquakes
Among his molehills, can adjust his telly
And drive him safely home—or wherever
He wants—so I watch the roles gradually
Reverse till mere oblivion over-
Takes all of us, sometimes surprising us
At extremely inconvenient hours.
Old age, however much an incubus,
Is a better alternative than flowers.
We live on memories of what we were
Trusting our young will opt to remember.

V.

Not from the stars do I my judgement pluck—
I married you because you trusted me:
Like Ruth, you made your choice and now you're stuck
Between the devil and the deep, blue sea.
I don't think you've ever been 'sick for home'
Because you've made these Yorkshire moors your place;
You know the footpaths when your urge to roam
Can lead you far from your accustomed space.
What we don't know is what we each would do
Without the other: wander aimlessly
Or find a raison d'être. 'The worst,' it's true,
'Is not so long'—as Edgar says—'as we
Can say "This is the worst."' I can't conceive,
Without you, how I would begin to live.

VI.

When I do count the clock that tells the time
I hear his wingèd chariot hurrying:
I think of all those subjects that my rhyme
Might compass, all our journeys, people, things
We've done and might redo. I know your best
Always emerges when the chips are down:
Almost as if our humdrum life lacked interest
You thrive on crises. Well I know your brown
Study face of boredom and 'Mum's death stare'
As it's been called. And then the sudden smile,
The lightning glance to tell me 'I'm aware—
Don't worry'. Subterfuge is not your style—
You're straight, uncomplicated as I know
Blest as I've been by fortune here below.

10. *Il faut cultiver nos jardins*

Some mid-Victorian called Brown only appears
In the Oxford Book of Quotations as author
Of one that starts 'A garden is a lovesome thing'.
By that time, certainly, his garden had replaced
His castle as the Englishman's true home. It might
Have started with Marvell as a subject-matter
Which you can trace through the ornamented measures
Of Pope while admiring the grandeur of Blenheim
Or Stowe. By the eighteenth century's end, the cult
Of leaving things to run wild was over-taking
Formality. One wonders what kind of garden
Voltaire was thinking we should be cultivating?
One imagines a potager, remembering
He spent three years in England but it's difficult
Not to picture Le Nôtre's vast parterres and fountains.

When we retired to a ground-floor flat I became,
Involuntarily, the sole proprietor
Of a 'petit jardin' (my wife's term—she never
Sets foot in it) which has an astonishing range:
Trees, shrubs and flowers with which I became acquainted
On an ad hoc basis when the weather was fine.
I had to make war on the two lawns' crop of weeds,
The dandelions, docks, daisies and mauvaises herbes
Or more fearsome varieties like ground elder.
There were roses to prune and two Leylandii trees
To chop down, a crab-apple to demould, olive
Trees to be sheltered, a tamarisk encouraged.
The more I did, the more I discovered things which
Had to be done, found new spaces to develop.

It was difficult also to limit oneself to
Working short periods, to judge how many plants
Were needed to fill empty spaces, to decide
On priorities on a particular day.
I also learnt that it wasn't much use asking
Other gardeners for advice as answers to
The same question usually contradicted each
Other. I think one of the reasons I enjoyed
Myself is that I never became addicted
Or pretended to any enthusiasm.
But I regret my need now for professional help
Just when it seemed that though I would never be good
At it, I had begun to understand Voltaire.

11. *D.o.b. 1936 Afterthoughts*

Being checked by the nurse, I heard the new patient's answer
To 'Religion?' and his explanation—'I'm a vicar':
How strange that even now he saw no need for 'Anglican'.
I ought not to have been listening – but the assumption
That there was only one kind of vicar obviously
Seemed an anachronistic lapsus which transported me
Back to my childhood and the reality of Empire.
Or, even further, to Coleridge and his Devonshire
Youth and ineradicable C. of E. certainties
Which always seem to constrain his pertinent enquiries
Despite that Broad Church movement—his own unique
                                    monument—
Which has outlasted most of his poems. Inconscient,
Unaware of my eavesdropping, my vicar, more fragile
Than I was, made his escorted progress down the ward aisle
Without so much as a nod in my direction
Which, on looking back, was a regrettable omission
On both our parts. We might have found something to talk about
In those unmistakable cut-glass accents which raise doubts
And suspicions in everybody else's minds.
As 'special category aliens', he and his kind
Were luckier than I: a Rev was expected to talk
That way but I was not—my speech a barrier to baulk
At as soon as I spoke. The Barbarians were a Greek
Concept comprehending peoples whose demotic unspeak
Defeated their efforts at real communication
But I don't think it was intended as derogation
Originally—merely a word like bibble-babble
And only much later denoting the common rabble,
By which stage one suspects it must have held some arrogance.
One thinks of Kipling's 'Recessional' as an instance
Of a foreboding late Victorian warning his peers

154

And, maybe, of how our grandparents thought a hundred years
  Ago. Yet accent still remains a gulf, unbridgeably
  Gaping within the very fabric of society.

12. Do you know where we're going?

I would like to think that, sometime in the future,
They will scatter our ashes among the heather
And gorse near the Sledgates trig point where my brother's
Remains lie but I have to reassure

You about your freedom to choose. The view
Over to Ravenscar is something we
Took for granted for well over thirty
Years but maybe it's not a rendez-vous

That you still want to keep. I picture you
By the Danby beacon, crossing the Esk
Via footbridge and ford. The picaresque
Element in your rambles could lead to

Strange discoveries—lime kilns and Bronze Age
Artefacts, tumuli, moorland crosses,
Great rolling vistas of bog mosses,
Peat, ling, rushes and scanty pasturage

For Blackface and Golden Plover. You know
A Peewit's a Lapwing a Green Plover,
Can distinguish between rabbit and hare,
Find seats overlooking Sandsend where you go

To relax after traversing the woods
Near those teashops with real home-made cooking.

What's to come is still unsure but looking
Ahead, be assured—whatever you would,

It will, in Shakespeare's phrase 'still better what
Is done'. According to Andromache,
Life with Hector was not all that easy:
They argued on principle and when not

Even sure of their facts. 'Like cat and dog'
Our eldest lately described us to Nurse Jo.
Time will say nothing but 'I told you'. So
Do what you will, enjoy the epilogue.

Active Decay
(2015)

Envoi

I watched the albatross with lazy wing
Shifting an inch of secondary to port,
Planing the combers and only missing
Their spray by a fraction. In a transport
Of grace, it veered to starboard, avoiding
The next breaker, laying itself athwart
The sea breeze, eventually soaring
Beyond our sight and naturally I thought

Of Baudelaire and Coleridge. To try
To recollect 'Souvent pour s'amuser'
Without a single French anthology
Within a thousand miles is just the way
To pass a South Atlantic afternoon
Or sleepless night under a Teesside moon.

For Nicky

We have delegated your little brother to visit
To-day. He will come, full of bonhomie,
Exuding charm to the nurses and instantly ready
With a bon mot or a quip to make you laugh;
Sometimes, I think, he is probably
A better visitor than we because he understands
Your processes of thought instinctively, quite apart
From knowing the jargon. Since I have been in hospital
And have been cast up, sleepless, on the wrecked beach
Of my own resources, I have often wondered where
You go in your dreams or what you think about,
My beamish boy, faced with the vast vacuity
Of teenage smut from the continuous telly
And eating battered cod for lunch on Fridays.
Have I been, maybe, to the same places, unknowing:
Vast and limitless lemon-gold beaches where I have been
Before but still never know what to expect apart
From acres and acres of premium ice-cream tubs:
Some day we must meet there and share one.

How to tell catkins from pussy-willow

The gaps in our broad-leaved belts of so-called
Native varieties become more clear:
Elms grow solitarily or in small
Clumps but when entire ash-groves disappear

You can't help noticing and it's easy
To miss the feathery green-white flowers
Of survivors. It seems the ash species
Grow like weeds yet I'd like to empower

Them with something to make them grow faster:
Tall oaks from little acorns grow but that
Takes time, in some cases, a thousand years—
Whereas the most ash (Yggdrasil apart)

Reach is maybe three hundred or, roughly,
The same as the oldest beech (there's a hedge
Somewhere in France with claims apparently
To be a lot older). Trees with the edge

When I was young were hazel and sallow
Because they both had catkins which we could
Gather in early spring, hacking hedgerow
And beckside with pen-knives, scouring the woods

For primrose and bluebell, and the meadows
For poppies, cornflower and scabious
With the half-colours of a hundred also-
Rans. It was odd things that could excite us

Like the first tuft of cowslips I chanced on
In a field not fifty yards from our door

Or the harebells ringing their silent notes
Beside the sheeptracks of the Goathland moor.

Heather we took for granted—but we knew
Enough to identify the bilberries,
Bog myrtle, cottongrass and sheep's-fescue,
The sphagnum mosses, scattered with sedges.

We knew that in high summer we had to
Look out for adders and, in autumn, where
To find conkers, at Christmas, mistletoe
And holly. The year's rites which, it seemed, were

Immutable, what everybody knows—
As we knew the twelve days of Christmas or
How to tell catkins from pussy willow—
Not at all what you might call useful info . . .

'Invited to apply'

Suppose I had gone ahead with the application,
Despite your veto, squeezing a left-hand foot
Into a right-hand shoe? When the chips were down
I had to be honest with myself about my agnosticism,
Even if I were to cite 'my career' as an ultimate
Persuader (not to speak of the 'gelt' which would have put you
Among the people your mother regarded as 'bien'). I can't
Imagine you dealing with Anglican bishops, anymore
Than I can see myself bearing false witness.

By then I had been running my own show
For over a dozen years and nobody doubted
That the place was alive and kicking. What kept me sane
Was the possibility of beginning to teach my own subject,
Though I remain grateful for my growing command
Of Nineteenth-Century European History and awareness
Of when one needed the Pluperfect Subjunctive.
The children, I think, were happy and the house
Was invariably overflowing spare pupils and dogs.

Those five or six years had some remarkable successes
Which seem to have passed unnoticed at the time:
The odd pupils were getting places at Oxbridge
And getting picked for the country as well as the county.
I would go to Headmasters' Conferences once or twice
A year and know that I would be known, as well as
Becoming aware that, thanks to my non-academic
Partner, I was teaching twenty-four more classes
A week than any of my colleagues.
I was meeting more of them because the English syllabus
Was 100% course-work which, within limits,
We were allowed to choose and modify ourselves.

It was a time when the workload could be truly excessive
But was also crowned with 100% pass rates
Though yet again, nobody seemed to notice outside
The classroom. The joys of schoolmastering
Are vicarious, I suspect more particularly when
One is self-educated in one's accidental trade.

Looking back, over twenty years later, I suppose
You did me a favour. I try to imagine myself
Preaching a sermon in chapel and marvel at what
Might have been the reaction, without having an idea
As to what I might possibly have said.
God knows that by then I had twelve years of material
To pick from, all of which would have been
New to those gallant sons of the middle-classes
And given the shade of Canon Woodard a bit of a fright.

The Naming of Birds

There is nothing logical about bird nomenclature
Though you have to discount Golden Orioles and forget
Blackbirds. Aged eleven, it would give me endless pleasure
To recite names: Curlew, Whimbrel, Greenshank, Kildeer, Egret—
And picture them on the moor, wondering which Jute or Dane
Originally dubbed the Kildeer and why? The answer's
The call (like the Kittiwake) which also helps to explain
Hosts of waders covered by the generic 'sandpipers'.

But why 'Purple' Sandpiper? Anything more like slate-grey
Is difficult to imagine but how often does one
Get a prolonged view? Presumably there's something to say
For a Yellow Wagtail being yellower than its cousin
Though the greyness has a hard struggle to predominate.
The more you come to consider, the more you are tempted
To indulge in lists of magical names. The alternates
Can tempt you further so that in Shetland you find listed

The Sandy-Loo, the Raingoose, the Tystie and the Maali
Only to discover Ringed Plover, Red-throated Diver,
Black Guillemot and Fulmar hiding behind the Bonxie
Which give you embarras de choix and often you prefer.
How do you separate the Brent, Barnacle and Bean Geese?
—Two small black jobs and a big grey? How barnacles grew
In Dark Age myth and beans developed into goose varieties
Are matters for men like Edward Topsell to delve into.

Crossing the Moor

Intelligent use of valley hill routes
—Don't even try calling them 'cols' round here —
Means you can access by car or on foot,
If necessary, anytime of year.

The four or five ways of crossing the moor
Are the roads people talk about. Birk Brow
Is usually first to close its door,
Then Skelder and Lockwood Beck—the trick now

Is to get up Horcum or Harewood Dale
Before they too are blocked. There were winters
Isolating us for weeks overall
On the moors but not the old panniers

Which obstinately gave safe passage to
Locals who knew their way about. To-day
Jim is taking me to hospital, so
I'm cocooned in straps and foam underlay,

Crossing the moor in June sunshine, noting
The care he is taking on the rough road
And mentally listing, remembering
Cricket grounds, pubs, orienteering modes

And melées of fox-hunts in teenage years.
This hill is the clod which giant Horcum
Lobbed at his girlfriend Siss with bitter jeers.
Here we fished rainbows till our hands went numb.

There's a Kestrel floating athwart the spinneys
Of larch and heather; five straining Greylags

Landing on Scaling, rich in memories
Of Osprey, Marsh Harrier and three Shags

Inexplicably straddling a bare bough
On the grey flood. I'd like to tread the cotton grass,
Pick some juniper, have a beer—but now?
No longer so easy as kiss your ass . . .

Bedtime with Bach

These days, I think about bed-time with love
And apprehension, never knowing how
My five or six hours will pan out or if
I will get three hours sleep – I don't mind now
Because effectively I ditch pretence
By day-napping between poems, crosswords
(I'm losing the knack) and correspondence:
Visitors take pot luck, help to feed birds.
It's a twenty-four hour day in which I look
Forward to bed-time and the cantaten
Of Bach which are next in the table-book
And I work my way through the collection.

It's music dropped straight from Elysia
Through which one floats in duet, melody
But, earthwise, Saxony, Thuringia
With folk-songs, country dances liberally
Scattered to leaven the more stately themes;
Some I play three times, some once is enough:
Always the sense of discovery, dreams
Of undiscovered countries mixed with bluff
Realities of peasant tunes. I kip
For twenty minutes, reawake, replay,
Then turn off everything for real sleep
Or that's the plan. Sometimes it lasts till day.

Springwatch

Both in sharp focus, the solid bourgeois
Sheldrake lumbered in front of the mincing
Ethereal avocet. The knowhow
Said 'Greenfinches' on the programme listing
Below but 'Springwatch' is full of surprise
As it is of delight and true wonder,
Which is as it should be for children's eyes
Or septuagenarian plunder.

I must have been twelve when we found our dear
Owl chicks—spitting balls of fluff which survived
Our manhandling—thirteen the blackcap year
When we knew better and only observed.
I rewind the stoats of my childhood
Undulating through Mount Grace Priory
And, equally, roaming in the Wild Wood,
Which has equal reality for me

Because, in those days, certainly it had,
(And I think this was shared by my fellows)
Though it was not something you paraded
And Public School tolled its foreclose—
After which one did not communicate.
Sheldrake and avocet when all is done
Are two more aspects of a changing state
Evolving to what strange communion?

Yorkshire v. Middlesex 9th June 2015

One burrows and wriggles right-angular
Into the National Health sofa pillow—
Comfort achieved, I need not go further:
The telephone invariably will go

And tear me away from the cricket score
Which ticks over, relentless, silently
To a hundred and twenty-six for four.
Relief comes from checking other counties

And while I've checked another wicket's gone.
I'd like to be at Headingley again
On some imagined warm June afternoon
But I don't think it's going to happen.

Middlesbrough Aubade

Chattering helicopter blades raise gulls
In panic from urban roofs. I awake
To their raucous clamour and, wakeful
One sleepless hospital night, start to shake

Out skeins of childhood memories. The war,
Which occupied most of my early days,
Drove all our Whitby cliff birds to harbour
On town roofs without searchlights and AAs—

So my little piece of cake soaked in tea
Is a harsh screaming 'awa awa' yell
Like kids down the street. Or I picture me
My grandmother's piano, tinkling bells

From the earlier war she didn't want
To remember. She would sing us ballads,
Folksongs, music hall numbers and ancient
Hits like 'Showboat', 'Jealousy'. And grandad

Would ask her to sing 'Polly Oliver'.
The gulls raise a further cacophony
Of screeches with wingbeats as another
Casualty comes back to earth safely.

Sestina in memory of Lucy Gray

She'd done some nanny jobs before: now, as mother,
What she remembered were her parting words to twin:
'I'll be his mother but I'm twenty-four years old,
I can't spend all my days being his guardian
But till the right man comes, that's my condition,
Until then I'll love and cherish him with my life.'

Sixteen years later, when she married, where was twin?
Still in Africa, helping Father run the old
Gold Coast. My brother and I were at our guardian's
Wedding with all our clan and where Aunt's conditions
Would be fulfilled with a man she cherished for life
As, after his death, she cherished our grandmother,

Who lived conveniently close, to the ripe old
Age of ninety. That was when *they* needed guardians,
My aunt and mother demanding home conditions
Independent of each other, not seeing life
In the real, nor managing, like their mother
To die at home but going inside a year, twin

After twin. By then I was nearly a guardian
But only as much as their own strict conditions
Allowed and constrained by my professional life—
I missed Aunt Lucy's death as I missed my mother's
But had Fauré's Pie Jesu played for each twin
And realised later how I was getting old.

It's since the diagnosis of my condition
That I've thought of those who've loved me during my life
Seriously, as did, I knew, my grandmother.
You would think that the loves of identical twins

Would be similar but that's another tale told
By an idiot. Dear Godmother and Guardian

How I wish I had been more kind to you in life
As I certainly tried to be to my mother
Whose inheritance paid for the home of her twin,
Where we too have to become used to growing old
But surrounded by children, grandchildren, guardians
Of our condition, our too human condition . . .

My aunt and deputy-mother, my mother's twin,
When I was six months old, became my guardian
And loved me without condition all through my life.

Visitors I

I look forward to visiting sessions
As a break in the routine every day
But, when you come, all I do is to grin
Inanely and take your hand, to convey

Without words—those mean old words—that, maybe
Unconditional, feeling of love for
Another person one's been used to see
For most of your life. Here, altogether,

I've been two months —this stay will be longest
I know but am also aware only
That exceptional circumstances
Will stop you coming across to see me

By bus, cab, friend, braving the moor –
And if you can't come, you'll do your damnedest
To chivvy one of our children over
In your place. They too have done their utmost,

Both girl and boys quite companionably
Holding my hand and ignoring the strange
Looks from foreign Anglo-Saxons for we
Are Franco-British (and watch it, Farage . . .)

Visitors II

As a bad visitor of the sick, I marvelled
At my family's daily comings and goings
Though soon the time we sat in agreeable
Silence outweighed chat and stealthy perusal
Of the dailies' sports news became habitual.
Unexpected nephew Jason, from New Zealand,
Was on a flying trip which boosted my morale,
Though this was probably not evident just then.
Our friend, associate and near-neighbour, Lucy came
Over once and, as I shall see her quite soon, I'm
Sorry for all the other old men who won't but
Who sat up and took notice when she crossed the ward,
Brightening our day, before driving Sylvie home.
The one I did not recognise was one who came
Outside visiting hours but was far too well-dressed
To be a doctor. When Mike told me who he was
I was delighted that the son of our old friends
Should have bothered to break his journey,
Assuming that, as a Surgery Professor,
He had pulled rank to get in but, smilingly,
He assured me he was incognito, having
Merely asked at Reception if he could see me.
We chatted an hour – scarcely enough to cover
A fifteen-year gap but renewing our bonds
Of family friendship fairly indelibly.
Sadie, my one-time pupil, friend and gardener,
Came out of hours too and also seemed to excite
My fellow-patients, who have formed a totally
False impression of my domestic circumstance …

Ward Curtain

I hardly noticed at first. Pale green
Masses streaked with blue strips and dotted with
Half-ruined buildings resolved themselves in
To places I knew from childhood and myth.

Once blues and greens became rivers and moors
The other pastel shades which emerged were
Pink and lemon. There were only these four
Hues I could painstakingly discover

But out of them grew Stockton and Whitby,
Transporter Bridge, Statue and Monument
To Cook and the Locomotive, Abbey,
Cathedral and Priory—testaments

To the capitalist economy
Of the Renaissance, the industrial
Alum Revolution based on Whitby
In a landscape based on *Das Kapital*—

Very far from the National Parks and days
By the seaside. In six months I have learnt
To trace and identify all the ways
And places round my home from one curtain.

Procedure

Midnight, and wheelchairs rattle the segments
In main corridor's floor which makes you realise
How fast the porters are pushing patients
As they traverse the hygienic, aseptic, aisles.

The clackety-clack blends with their greetings
But lacks the day's hum. The theatre,
More like a thirties' cinema with sweeping
Curves and softly buzzing machinery,

Might well overawe but for the presence
Of friendly surgeon and nurses, at pains
To explain everything except the tense
Knot in my gut which frees itself and drains

Away as the anaesthetic takes hold.
We talk of holidays and if it's right
To go with grandparents, kids, and uphold
Family values or, exert your right

And go solo to Tristan da Cunha,
Like me or, like Sylvie, to take a trip
And do solo the Great Wall of China.
The operation ends with one more snip.

Dream 1

Did I really sit in one of the salons of the Vichy
Club du Parc while making polite conversation
With genuine representatives of the NHS? Fifty-odd
Years before, I had been working in the Pavillon Sévigné,
The distinguished hôtel next door, where employees
Would not have sullied their feet in the carpets of the reputed
Maison de passe. Now, by God, an English doctor
I knew by name nodded his recognition at me
And I was relieved to see him. Though half my being
Was telling me that the renowned Vichy medical school
Had been taken over by the James Cook Memorial Hospital
In Teesside, the other half was nevertheless
Still telling me that actually what I was doing was lying
In Ward Seven of that same Middlesbrough hospital.

Dream 2

Somewhere, perhaps in the Nice Côte d'Azur Region,
Moving among the artistic circles with lots
Of distant relations, friends who painted and potted,
Filled books with paintings of two-toned bowls
Holding semi-circular flowers and put up pictures
On every possible wall, I mingled with other jetsam
Of the sixties, writing strange music for hammerless
Harpsichords, above all keeping out of their way.

Then it was Feast Day with a procession
Of altar boys swinging censers, smells of garlic
And wine, brass bands, tumpity-tump, and candles
In all the windows, exaggerating the height
Of the houses. It was something of a Walpurgis night
And I went on keeping out of people's way
Until everything went sour and widdershins
And suddenly all I knew was that I had to
Keep the wires up my nose and that somewhere
There had to be a bed where I could lie down and rest.

Dream 3 : Daleside Castle Library

I had been here before—was it thirty
Years ago?—looking at first editions
—Incunabula as well as Brontës
And Dickens – these last in good condition

But the former half-encased in white grime.
I don't understand why we're sleeping here,
Me and my fellow-bibliophiles—I'm
Stuck at a corridor end in nightwear

And a learned expert says the white stuff
Can't be removed so don't waste time on them:
But I cannot remember half enough—
The threats are nameless and unease the same—

How did it end I wonder? Not in fire,
That would have been too easy. Rot and mould
Pervaded priceless tomes—the antiquaire
Lectured on myrrh and frankincense and gold.

Dream 4 : Reverie Balzacienne

There's one of the 'Comedie Humaine' where Balzac
Decides to organise a confrontation of powers
Involving the financiers/politicals—even
Royalty and the military I seem to remember,
As I do Rastignac playing a key-role offstage
And Lucien de Rubempré noticeably absent.

What is interesting about the July Monarchy
Is its resemblance to post-Dissolution
England, when a whole new class of ruthless buccaneers
Bought Church property cheap and held on to it
Through enough generations to make their families
An unremovable part of the status quo.

I'm not sure why I and my family should have been
Engaged in some sort of coup in Paris
Under Louis-Philippe but I know they had to be all
In different places at the same time in order
To play their rôles and je me souviens de
Madame de Veit qui venait exactement à l'heure juste

To make her bid for the masterpiece. Our daughter
Then disappeared and I glimpsed milord Peter
Waving a damascene blade before he too
Vanished into the realms of fantasy, holding
My family speechless for a hallucinogenic
Night, of which Simon, the eldest, still won't talk to me.

A Walk with Caroline

Arguing with the Physio ladies is pointless
—In the nicest possible manner they will
Indicate how much better you will feel
After a stroll through the corridors, bedecked
With half-full catheters and pushing a pylon
On wheels. Occasionally Caroline puts out
A hand to retrain my billowing gown – it's
Curious how a sense of pudeur seems to pervade
The hospital though in a rare one-to-one
Situation the conversation can flow into
Unusual channels. I learnt to-day that Caroline
Has three children who all love raw salad dishes;
She learnt that our four children loved a pork
(Four or five varieties) and lentil stew
Which could last three days in various guises.
This change from lying in bed so emboldens me
That I ask the Registrar why the tricolore
Is not flying over the ward for it is,
After all, le quatorze Juillet and Vive la France!

Another Springwatch

The Cetti's Warbler's nest seems empty though
The sign says 'Live'. If the nestlings are there,
It seems strange they continue to lie low
For so long. I switch channels, turn over
And back to find more Greenfinches fledging
Before coming back to the humming scrape,
Alive with Redshank, Scaup and Sanderling,
Gleaning and probing the rich waterscape.

I suppose I could tell Redshank before
I was eleven because I had seen
Some live ones. Was I therefore luckier
Than my grandson who has watched them on screen?

Another Cantata

To the artist the blank page is a temptation,
An invitation to a dance wherein messages
Are yet unwritten (guessed at by Matisse and Yeats),
Flickering on horizons of our consciousness
And luring us helplessly into the banal
Chant or folklorique ditty which, in its substance,
Answered the need triumphantly as far as Bach
Was concerned. We have to marvel at the sheer weight
Of the work he accomplished, quality apart.
One is tempted to wonder if he was trying
To compensate for the unpitying sermon
With a paean of melodies praising the Lord.

NOTES

THE ART-FORM called 'The Poem with notes' is a modern phenomenon. If these poems do not work without notes, they probably don't work. However, having listened to the queries of friends (there's a phenomenon) whose opinion I value, here are some facts which readers may or may not find useful.

Variations on Familiar Themes

The Marmottan Revisited 2011
The Marmottan is a Museum/Gallery on the edge of the Bois de Boulogne and rather off the beaten track of the Parisian tourist. Its most noteable asset is a collection of paintings by Claude Monet. It has three floors, of which the underground one is entirely devoted to large Monet works.
Les Nymphéas. Monet did a considerable number of large paintings of water-lilies. Two or three are in the Marmottan.
In 1981, Peter Woolley was 10. His grandfather, Pierre François was 74. So was John Woolley in 2011.
The Japanese bridge at Giverny was another subject that Monet painted many times.
Impression, soleil levant', dated 1872, is perhaps the most famous single item in the Museum.
Delacroix developed a new way of painting water using dots of basic colours c.1825.
'Visible' is pronounced as in French, ie: two syllables, not three.
The stanza form is one used by Yeats—the last line recalls the last line of 'Among Schoolchildren'.

Deux de la Vague
Title—the name of a film about Truffaut and Godard which came out in December 2010/January 2011. The French *cinéastes* of the late 1950s/early 1960s were known as La Nouvelle Vague.
Ouvreuses = Usherettes

Madeleine. Eating a little cake called a madeleine made Proust remember his childhood and write sixteen volumes about it.
Skull-cinema—a phrase invented (I think) by the late John Hillaby.
Names of films:

Jules et Jim	(Truffaut)
À bout de souffle	(Godard)
Tirez sur le Pianiste	(Truffaut)
North by Northwest	(Hitchcock)
Les Quatre Cents Coups	(Truffaut)
La Dolce Vita	(Fellini)
L'Avventura	(Antonioni)
La Notte	(Antonioni)
Nuits et Brouillards	(Resnais)
Hiroshima mon Amour	(Resnais)
La Nuit Americaine	(Truffaut)

Vitti—Monica Vitti was the star of *L'Avventura*.
Nevers—the administrative centre of a département in the middle of France.
Like Keats's—see 'The Eve of St Agnes' Stanza XLII, line 2
The petrichor—A pleasant, distinctive smell that often accompanies the first rain after a long period of warm, dry weather …
the last tycoon—see *The Last Tycoon* by F. Scott Fitzgerald (Penguin edition, p. 40).

Land of the Troubadours
In the Long Vac of 1959 at Cambridge I was given a travel scholarship (£30) to go and look at the Romanesque architecture in the triangle formed roughly by Perigueux, Bergerac and Limoges. I think the original version of this poem was written in the railway station of the latter city, where I was awaiting a train back to Paris, having lived for three weeks on the bounty of Christ's College.

De Gaulle had returned to power in May 1958—the political climate in France in the summer of 1959 was fluctuating, to put it mildly.

Reading Proust in a punt near Grantchester.
line 5—'not green nor deep.' See R. Brooke 'The Old Vicarage, Grantchester', line 10.
line 10—*The Allegory of Love* is a book by C. S. Lewis, Professor of Medieval & Renaissance Literature at Cambridge in 1957.
lines 11/12—modifications of quotations from Proust but the pages generally referred to in this poem come towards the end of the section called 'Combray' in *Du Côté de Chez Swann*.
lines 19-21—See Shakespeare's Sonnet 5 and Sidney's *Arcadia* from which Shakespeare apparently swiped the image.
line 32—Joseph Needham. The first volumes of *Science and Civilisation in China* started to appear in 1954.
line 34—Reviewing SCC in 1973, George Steiner compared it to *À la Recherche du Temps Perdu* using these terms.

An Education 1954
line 1—*The Magic Flute*
line 14—the Bloedput is one of the old city gates
line 16—Virgil was Dante's guide through Hell and Purgatory
lines 45/46—See 'Frater Ave atque Vale', Tennyson on Sirmio and 'The Scholars', Yeats on Catullus
line 50— San Zeno is the church in Verona which houses the shrine of its patron saint
line 58—the Warsaw Concerto was the theme music of a film called 'Dangerous Moonlight'.
line 61—uneven paving-stones were one of the factors which triggered Proust's memories of Venice in 'Le Temps Retrouvé'
line 63—the Badia is a church in Venice
line 65— the Scrovegni chapel in Padua has frescoes by Giotto.
line 71—cf: *Paradise Lost* Book 1, line 289
line 87—San Domenico is a church in Fiesole

line 88—the Palio is a horse race round the square of Siena
line 91—Divine Comedy: Paradise, Canto X ll: 58 ff
line 95—*The Birth of Venus* by Botticelli
line 96—The San Lorenzo Chapel houses the Medici tombs by Michelangelo
Place Names
The poem is a series of notes and vice versa.
Oradour-sur-Glane was the scene of a particularly nasty Nazi massacre in 1944.

Ronas Voe
Ronas is the highest hill in Shetland. It is situated in the NW corner of Shetland Mainland. Immediately to its South is Ronas Voe, an inlet which nearly cuts the Mainland in half.
Gavin Douglas (1475?–1522?) was a Scots poet, linked to a group loosely known as the Scottish Chaucerians. He graduated from St Andrews and probably studied in Paris. He says he completed his translation of Virgil's *Aeneid,* each book with his own Prologue, in 1513. He became Bishop of Dunkeld in 1515 and immediately got involved in politics, which led to his temporary imprisonment. Sent on a mission to London, he was accused of high treason and died in exile, possibly of the Plague.
Palamedes was credited with the invention of the Greek alphabet, having studied the shapes made in the sky by the flight of cranes. See G. Douglas Prologue to Bk.VII 1: 119.
Gabriel hounds = Wild geese (Whitby Glossary 1876 – OED)
tell court huntsmen … See J. Donne 'The Sun Rising', verse 1.
Your face in mine eye … See J. Donne 'The Good-Morrow' verse 3.
Sonnet 7—See 'Le Sous-Préfet dans les Champs', A. Daudet *Lettres de Mon Moulin*
raingoose = the Shetland name for Red-throated Diver
Wet in the mindless flood of Hell, Lethe. *Aeneid* Book V 1.854
Sonnet 10–11: 4-6—these are adapted from odd lines in Douglas's Prologues. Line 9 cf: 'What is the price of experience . . .' (William Blake, *Vala, or the Four Zoas.*)

Love-letter for Jeanne-Marie

Mortemart—the family name of Madame de Montespan before she married the Marquis de Montespan. She was the favourite of Louis XIV for a considerable time—long enough to have eight children by him.

C'est une honte = How shameful.

C'est scandaleux = It's a scandal.

Tu as tort = You're wrong (lit: You have wrong).

St Elizabeth de Hongrie. She, disobeying her husband, the King's commands, had been carrying food to the poor—an apron full of bread—when her husband saw her.

'What have you in your apron?' he demanded.

'Roses,' lied St. Elizabeth.

'Show me,' said her husband.

St. Elizabeth showed him, and her apron was full of roses.

Oui, je m'en souviens = Yes, I remember

The Delacroix Museum is in the Place de Furstenberg (in between the Boulevard St Germain and the rue Jacob).

'Plus Belle la Vie' is the French equivalent of 'Neighbours'.

Attention! Cela continue...' = Be careful! It goes on …

Clarissa (1747–49), an epistolary novel by Samuel Richardson, in nine volumes.

Proust. The first edition of *À la Recherche du Temps Perdu* was in sixteen volumes.

Le pauvre homme = Poor fellow (Orgon in *Le Tartuffe*)

'Faut-il qu'il m'en souvienne / La joie'. (Guillaume Apollinaire, 'Le pont Mirabeau', first verse).

Le Père Lachaise. The cemetery on the West side of Paris where many famous people are buried, including Abelard and Heloise, Chopin, Molière, Edith Piaf, Balzac, Proust, Apollinaire and Delacroix. And Jeanne-Marie.

Rastignac At the end of Balzac's 'Le Père Goriot' the young hero, Rastignac, alone after the burial in le Père Lachaise of old Goriot (which his beloved daughters have failed to attend), looks out over Paris and proclaims: 'Now it's between you and me!'

Spectator
The Greek philosopher Pythagoras observed that there are three kinds of people in life, just as there are three kinds of people who go to the Olympic Games.
At the lowest level are those who go to buy and sell.
Above them are those who go to compete.
Highest of all, however, are those who go simply to look on.

Imperfections 2013

II. John likes water
Stanza 1, line 1—'ram': 'an automatic water-raising machine in which the raising power is supplied by the concussion of a descending body of water in a pipe.' (O.E.D.)
> line 3 'dam': lower side of pool below waterfall.
> line 4 'foss': waterfall

Awkward Age 1946
Title. My tenth birthday was in September 1946
Stanza 3, line 1—'Grandfather': My grandfather, Arthur Woolley (1876-1945), was Surveyor to the North Riding of Yorkshire 1919-1945.

Alf and Uncle Robert
Stanza 8, line 4—'a roke': a fog ('probably of Scandinavian origin' O.E.D.)
Stanza 12, line 2—'ganseys': fishermen's jerseys. On the Yorkshire coast, each fishing settlement has its own complicated knitting pattern. This is to help in the identification of drowned bodies washed up by the sea.

Pinned on a wall in Verona
line 6—'mannerly devotion': Cf. *Romeo and Juliet*, I.v. line 97.

Mother Thekla

Stanza 3, line 7—'monastery': The Monastery of the Assumption, a Greek Orthodox monastery, was originally established by Mother Maria in the 1970s, with the active participation of Mother Katherine and Mother Thekla, in a converted farmhouse on the edge of the North Yorkshire Moors at High Normanby. It lasted for about thirty years but it has been deconsecrated and is now a private dwelling-place.

Andrew at the airport

Stanza 1, line 7—Cf. Milton 'On his blindness' line 14 and *The Tempest* III, ii, line 141.

Stanza 4, line 6—The headquarters of the Hong Kong and Shanghai Banking Corporation is in Gracechurch Street in the City of London.

Stanza 5, line 2—Kai Tak was still Hong Kong's International airport in 1982.

Stanza 8, line 2—Spurn Head is the southernmost tip of the East Riding of Yorkshire.

Line 4—Cape Palliser is the southernmost tip of the East coast of North Island, New Zealand.

Stanza 9, line 7—Cf. Shakespeare Sonnet XVIII, line 14.

Relativity

Stanza 3, line 2—'The Cretan glance':
'I feel something else, a synthesis, a being that not only gazes on the abyss without disintegrating, but which, on the contrary, is filled with coherence, pride, and manliness by such a vision. This glance which confronts life and death so bravely, I call Cretan.' Nikos Kazantzakis. See the Introduction to his '*The Odyssey: A Modern Sequel*' by the translator, Kimon Friar p: xlx.

Stanza 4, line 3—'the Spartan': Cf. A. E. Housman, 'The Oracles'.

II Huis Clos

Stanza 2, line 3 & 4—When Louis Philippe became King of the

French in 1830, his Prime Minister François Guizot, is credited with having advised citizens who wished to qualify for the franchise, 'Enrichissez-vous'.

Sestina from the Pontic Steppe
Stanza 1, line 1—William of Rubruk (1220-1293) was a Flemish Franciscan sent by Saint Louis (King of France) to the Great Khan whom he met in Karakorum, in Mongolia, having walked and ridden there, in 1254. Many historians regard his account of his travels as more veracious than Marco Polo's (1254-1324).

A Propos from Alain
Title. Alain: pseudonym of Emile Chartrier (1868-1951). Essayist and humanist philosopher.

Ballade of the last Englishman
Stanza 4, line 1—'lines from Flecker': among his Little Books, Carr published his own favourite, Flecker. In his original introduction, Carr stated:
'He wrote one memorable line—
          'Their bosoms shame the roses; their behinds
          Impel the astonished nightingales to sing.'
But then struck it out.
(See *The Last Englishman* by Byron Rogers 2003, p. 7.)

R.I.P.
Stanza 1, lines 2/3—See *A Stone in the Shade* by Lady Violet Powell (2013) pp. 103/4. She was, of course, not Lady Powell.
Stanza 5, line 1—Cf: e.e. Cummings 'my sweet old etcetera'.
line 3. My own Aunt Lucy was my mother's twin sister and my godmother.

Chain Reaction

II (The Suitors : Book I)
line 3—'the Starkadders' see Stella Gibbons's *Cold Comfort Farm*.

XII (the sere, the yellow leaf : Book XXIII)
Title see *Macbeth*, III i l: 23.

3. Sleeping out
line 8—'Fiesole'. A hilltop village outside Florence from which
Galileo used to view the stars (according to Milton).

5. Charon
line 10—Avon—the Hampshire one.

6. Jasmine and Ursula
for notes on Jasmine and Ursula, the 'clan mothers' or 'the seven
daughters of Eve' see Francis Prior *Britain BC*, pp 116-121.

9. On not reading Shakespeare's Sonnets in hospital—V
lines 11-13—*King Lear*, IV; ll: 27-28.

Active Decay

Envoi
line 10—'Souvent pour s'amuser' are the opening words of
Baudelaire's poem 'L'Albatros'.

Invited to apply
line 16—'the Pluperfect Subjunctive'. Following the publication
of another volume of *À la recherché du temps perdu* someone—I
think it was Gide—remarked to Proust 'I particularly admired
your use of the Pluperfect Subjunctive'.

line 45—'Canon Woodard'. Nathaniel Woodard (1811-1891) was the founder of the Woodard Schools. There are still quite a number of them for boys, such as Lancing, Hurstpierpoint and Ardingly in the South, Denstone, Worksop and Ellesmere in the Midlands and, for girls, such schools as Abbot's Bromley near Rugeley in Staffs and Queen Mary's in North Yorkshire.

The Naming of Birds
line 24—'Edward Topsell'. Topsell (1572-1625) was a London parson who had already compiled two large volumes on quadrupeds and on serpents before he embarked on 'The Fowles of Heaven'. He only got as far as those birds whose names began with A, B and C. (This ran to 248 leaves and 124 woodcuts).

Crossing the Moor
It is twenty-one miles by road in any direction from Whitby before you come to a town of equal size: to the North there is Guisborough, to the West, Pickering and to the South, Scarborough. It was in that triangle of countryside that I grew up.

Springwatch
line 13—'stoats' These were real ones which were still there relatively recently.
line 15—'the Wild Wood' These stoats came from *The Wind in the Willows*.

Middlesbrough Aubade
line 8—'AAs' Anti-Aircraft Guns
line 9—This line refers to how the taste of a little cake called a madeleine caused the adult Proust to start recollecting his childhood – at the beginning of his sixteen volume novel.

Ward Curtain
line 11—'the Locomotive' is the sculpture of 'Mallard' near Darlington which is built entirely of bricks.

Reverie Balzacienne
line 7—'the July Monarchy' The Orleans branch of the Bourbons
ruled France under Louis-Philippe (the richest man in France at
his accession) from 1830-1848.